THE
WAY
OF
FAITH

THE
WAY
OF
FAITH

40-DAY DEVOTIONAL

Allowing God to
Experience Us

T.W.S. HUNT

BroadStreet
PUBLISHING

BroadStreet Publishing Group, LLC
Racine, Wisconsin, USA
BroadStreetPublishing.com

THE WAY OF FAITH: *Allowing God to Experience Us*

ISBN-13: 978-1-4245-5429-4 (hardcover)
ISBN-13: 978-1-4245-5430-0 (e-book)

Stock or custom editions of BroadStreet Publishing titles may be purchased in bulk for educational, business, ministry, fundraising, or sales promotional use. For information, please e-mail info@broadstreetpublishing.com.

Cover design by Chris Garborg at garborgdesign.com
Typesetting by Katherine Lloyd at theDESKonline.com

Printed in China

17 18 19 20 21 5 4 3 2 1

To David John Parker,
who wanders along the way with me.

And for those who have served as way-finders:
Peter and Joanne, Cristin, Dave, Calvin, Penny,
Don, Brian, Sarah, and Paul

Contents

"Two roads diverged in a wood, and I—
I took the one less traveled by,
And that has made all the difference."

—*Robert Frost*, The Road Not Taken

Seeking Spiritual Spring

We know [God] in so far as we become aware of
ourselves as known through and through by him.

—*Thomas Merton,* Contemplative Prayer[1]

*T*he Way of Faith is about ways of being faithful to God,
and the ways in which God is faithful to us. But this book
promotes the idea that faith is what allows God to experience
us, rather than promising that faith shall enable us to experience God. It also maintains that the most important part of
our personal relationship with God is not the extent to which
we know God, but the extent to which God knows us. That
is, God's knowledge of us in the sense of intimacy and not
information, and relationship rather than rationality.

And it is with that in mind that *The Way of Faith* explores
the various stages and settings, as well as tensions and tussles, in which faith must survive—but can also thrive. All the
while making the case—sometimes explicitly but more often
implicitly—that however far away we might feel from God,

our continued faithfulness can allow God to feel that much closer to us.

The topics in this book vary as much as its sources. In these chapters you'll encounter thinkers both ancient and modern, ranging from Lucretius and St. Augustine to Søren Kierkegaard and Annie Dillard. You'll also read about everything from bereavement and benevolence to theology and time management. But it does not matter if you've read a lot or a little, if you have great faith or hardly any, or whether you belong to one church or to another (or to no church at all). This book was written for anyone with an open mind and an open heart.

Regarding the book itself, you will note that there is some springtime imagery sprinkled throughout the text. This is partly due to the fact that this book was composed in spring, and partly because *The Way of Faith*—in my mind—is an unofficial and partial sequel to my previous book, *Winter with God*. For where the latter did not presuppose an interest in discipleship, and therefore had to make a continual case for it, the former presupposes it so much as to not make any further mention of it: going from a kind of winter to spring.

My prayer for you is that the way of faith shall become a way of life. That things like faith, hope, and love, which, as Frederick Buechner said, "as words are so worn out," will become, "as realities so rich."[2] It is my hope that as much as you might come to know God, God shall come to know you even more. For it is God's knowledge of us, not our knowledge of God, that is stressed so highly as a criterion for determining our future fate (Matthew 7:21–23). But may you come to enjoy in heaven what you have longed for here on earth, because as Jesus said, "Now this is eternal life: that they know you, the only true God" (John 17:3).

Note to the Reader

*T*he Way of Faith can be read in many ways. It can be read in spurts and sprees, glacially and with gusto. The recommended approach, however, is to read this book both incrementally and intentionally: one chapter a day, with time and space to contemplate its contents. Read it slowly and surely, working your way through it like a river on its water-course, winding from one prayerful thought to another, being carried along by living waters until you make your way to the sea—and out into the great beyond.

The Long Winter

"But I lavish unfailing love for a thousand generations
on those who love me and obey my commands."

Exodus 20:6 NLT

Sometimes spring arrives early, and occasionally it comes late. In 1609, however, the season scarcely came at all for the fledgling colony of Quebec. In fact, spring might as well have not sprung, since the long winter claimed twenty of the colony's twenty-eight colonists. Yet the eventual arrival of spring did not mark the departure of the surviving eight, even though they knew that dysentery, scurvy, and starvation could strike again. Instead, the courageous eight amazingly remained, for they realized that the preservation of Quebec required the perseverance of its people.

There are seasons in the spiritual life when the calendar says spring, but it still feels like winter in the soul. Like the colonists in Quebec, we're surviving, but we're not thriving. Spiritually, we may be born again, but things somehow feel stillborn; there's faith but it feels lifeless, love but it seems lackluster, and hope but it all looks helpless. As in Quebec, we're trapped in winter, desperate for spring, but we're afraid that it might come too late.

At some point we must decide between passively plodding and actively persevering, because the choices we make in winter will shape the character we have in spring. For what we do in the hardest times, influences what we do all the time.

In Quebec, the colonists who bravely endured gave new life to the land by subsequently shaping its culture, language, architecture, and religion. Likewise, those who have kept the faith in even the harshest winters—like Joseph in prison, or David on the run—have blessed themselves and others with an even greater spring.

In winter, we owe it to ourselves to see the season through. "'For I know the plans I have for you,' declares the LORD, 'plans to prosper you ..., plans to give you hope and a future'" (Jeremiah 29:11). And we also owe it to others—to do them good rather than harm—because whatever we do for ourselves, we ultimately do to them: the caring provide care and the courageous give courage, but the bitter show bitterness and the despondent spread despair.

Most of all, however, we should keep faith with God, because God has kept faith with us. And it is precisely when life and faith are at their hardest—when a relationship with God feels the most impersonal to us—that our perseverance can make God's relationship with us feel all the more personal to him.

Application: What are the kindest words of encouragement you can give to yourself in order to preserve and promote your own faithfulness?

Supplication: Lord, might I give to you what I wish you would give to me, so long as I can see that whatever I have given to you was first of all given to me. For I have no faith to offer you apart from the faithfulness you have offered me. Thank you. Come, Holy Spirit. Amen.

2

To Have Faith, Be Faithful

"You will seek me and find me when you
seek me with your whole heart."

Jeremiah 29:13

Jesus told a parable about a father who had two sons. In it, the two sons were both asked to work in their father's vineyard. The first refused to do so but thereafter went to the vineyard and worked, whereas the second son said he would do so but never did. When the audience was asked which of the sons rightly honored the father's wishes, they correctly responded that it was the first son.

What we say matters, but what we do matters even more. This is not because actions speak louder than words; it's because actions are the truest words that can be spoken. We cannot truthfully call ourselves runners, for instance, without running; nor can we say that we are writers, unless we're actually writing. So too, our words of faith require works of faith in order to become genuinely faithful.

Leo Tolstoy wrote, "Where there is life, there is faith."[1] It could also be said that where there is faith, there must be life: the vital signs of vivacity, morality, and liberality. For there is more to a faith-life than just living faithfully, because we have to live with more than our belief in mind; we must live with others in mind. Indeed, it is the work of faith to become a labor of love, to turn us upward and outward, toward the good of God and others.

Just as love without faith is only a feeling, so faith without love is only fleeting. In fact, it's fatally ephemeral, as "faith without works is dead" (James 2:26 NASB). It is dead, because faith can only live and grow through love—the kind that loves to love in word and deed, which strives for the extraordinary but thrives in the ordinary. For it is love, and not faith, as Paul said, that actually "believes all things, [and] hopes all things" (1 Corinthians 13:7 ESV). It is love that separates true faith from mere belief, just as Jesus said it would be love that separated the sheep from the goats. Which is why Paul also said, "The only thing that counts is faith expressing itself through love" (Galatians 5:6).

We cannot grow our faith in God without greater love for God. Yet love isn't enlarged just by willing it, but also by wishing for it. For just as James wrote, "If any of you lacks wisdom, you should ask God … and it will be given to you" (James 1:5), so we can ask for love and likewise receive it. So let us ask for it, because our love for God can only come from our loving-God. Let us seek it, because our faith is measured by what we desire, not just what we do. And let us find it—thereby finding the love that always wanted to be found: God.

Application: Develop your faith by becoming more intentional about your love. To that end, plan to do something both pleasant and surprising for someone you would not normally love or whom you seldom find lovable.

Supplication: Lord, as blood flows through my body, may love flow through my faith. May there be neither belief without benevolence nor faith without fidelity. Come, Holy Spirit. Amen.

3

Faith after Failure

If you, LORD, kept a record of sins, LORD,
who could stand? But with you there is forgiveness.

Psalm 130:3–4

Sin is a constant source of embarrassment to faith, since it follows us around like a shadow, matching our moves and mirroring our identity. Likewise, sin can be discouraging, because it's nothing if not demoralizing to repent from a sin that we know we're likely to be—if not already—tempted to repeat. But repent we must, because sin cannot be redressed until it's been addressed, just as a sickness has to be revealed before it can be healed.

Fortunately, however much we lose the battle when we fall into temptation, we're still winning the war when we get back up—regardless of whether that takes us many times or a million. "For the LORD your God is he who goes with you to fight against your enemies, to give you the victory" (Deuteronomy 20:4 ESV).

To sin is to be amongst the saints. For there is not a hero amongst the faithful without a sinful flaw: like Abraham the coward, Sarah the disbeliever, David the adulterer, or Paul the persecutor. But if we are like the saints in sinning, let us not be unlike them in praying. For they understood that they could approach God—no matter how imperfectly, so long as they did so sincerely—because "we do not make requests of [God] because we are righteous, but because of [God's] great mercy" (Daniel 9:18). So when we sin, we can pray as they did, from this honest, earnest, and plaintive psalm:

> Have mercy on me, O God, according to your unfailing love; according to your great compassion blot out my transgressions. ... For I know my transgressions, and my sin is always before me. ... Cleanse me with hyssop, and I will be clean; wash me, and I will be whiter than snow. ... Create in me a pure heart ... and renew a steadfast spirit within me. Do not cast me from your presence or take your Holy Spirit from me. Restore to me the joy of your salvation and grant me a willing spirit. (Psalm 51:1–12)

Like these saints, let us also pray not only for the grace to be forgiven, but also for the grace to not need so much forgiveness. For there is help enough—so long as we seek it—to outdo the temptations that try to undo us. Because, as Paul said, "When you are tempted, [God] will show you a way out so that you can endure" (1 Corinthians 10:13 NLT). To do what is right, however, requires that we pray to be strong enough, not merely to hate evil but also to love what is good.

For love is a positive force, while hate—even hatred of what is hateful—can become in us a dark and dangerous thing. As Martin Luther King Jr. said, "Darkness cannot drive out darkness; only light can do that. Hate cannot drive out hate; only love can do that."[1] But even more than loving what is good, let us pray for an even greater love for God. Because love can enlighten us to how much our sin hurts the heart of God—so much so, it shall inspire us to sin less, simply because we do not want to hurt God more.

Application: The psalms are sung poetry. So the next time you sin, prayerfully listen to this song version of Psalm 51 by Jon Foreman, "White as Snow."

Supplication: God, between the longing not to hurt you and not hurting you stands a gap that my love so often seems unable to fill; so thank you that between my love for you and your love for me stands your Son and our Savior, Jesus Christ. Come, Holy Spirit. Amen.

4

Can a Desert Bloom?

O God … my soul thirsts for you.

Psalm 63:1 ESV

The Lord led a prophet into a valley filled with dry bones. It was a wasteland of wearied souls and ruined religion. Then the Lord asked him, "Son of man, can these bones live?" (Ezekiel 37:3). The prophet was not sure, and neither are we. For many of us have been in the valley as well—suffering from setbacks and struggles, delays and disappointments—so much so, we're unsure whether or not these bones can live or love again.

The Valley of Dry Bones is metaphorical, but Death Valley is literal. To envision the former, simply visit the latter. It's a scorched, sandy, wind-swept desert, stranded in the lowest, hottest, driest area in North America. It seems godforsaken, but like the Valley of Dry Bones, one believes that if hope can be found there, it can be found anywhere.

Most of the time, there is virtually nothing to be found in

Death Valley; but occasionally, the marvelous, if not miraculous, occurs. For when the rains have come, when the sun is hot and the winds are low, the entire valley can be raised from death to life. Then the hillsides bloom with wildflowers like desert mariposa, purple sage, and magnificent lupine; and the once-dead valley blushes vermillion, lavender, and canary gold.

When the Lord looked upon the dry bones, he said, "I will put my Spirit in you and you will live" (Ezekiel 37:14). So too, God looks upon our desert and wants it to flower. He wants to irrigate our hearts with living water so that we might bloom forever. "Indeed," Jesus said, "the water I give them will become in them a spring … welling up to eternal life" (John 4:14). It does not matter where we've been or what we've done; all we need to do is believe. Because, "Whoever believes in me," Jesus declared, "will never be thirsty" (John 6:35).

That isn't to say that nobody will ever be disappointed again, because many of us would prefer to be uprooted and replanted somewhere better than remain somewhere bitter. The fact that water can revive our parched hearts often does little to dissuade us, however, since hardship makes us want to be transferred somewhere desirable, instead of being transformed someplace deplorable. But grace often reshapes us before it relocates us, because who we are on the inside follows us wherever we go on the outside—and to bloom in a desert is to be able to bloom anywhere we might go.

Application: To witness how a life, like a valley, can be resuscitated from death to life, watch Terrence Malick's Palme d'Or-winning film, *The Tree of Life*.

Supplication: Lord, I want to live, but only as I would like; I want to be healthy, but only as I would be happy; and I want to have you, but only I do not want to be had. Help me, therefore, to accept your grace as it is given, in the spirit that it is sent, to the ends that you have ordained. Otherwise I shall never live as I was made to, care as I was called to, or enjoy life as I was created to. Come, Holy Spirit. Amen.

5

Beyond Me

"All the Law and the Prophets
hang on these two commandments."
Matthew 22:40

Let me not forget, that no matter
The love I have won and lost
Or never had at all:
True love is not
Beyond me

Remind me often, however much
I missed the point in the past
Or misread the present:
Knowledge is not
Beyond me

Help me to remember, whatever
The gains that I have wasted
Or lessons I've unlearnt:
Progress is not
Beyond me

And aid my memory, that even if
I have longed for the right
But lived in the wrong:
Goodness is not
Beyond me

For the best in life is still to come
When there's good to be done
In cherishing God and
Choosing another
Beyond me

This is goodness beyond measure
Love that's beyond pleasure
Riches beyond treasure
A life of adventure—
Beyond me

Application: The next time you feel potentially overwhelmed by something—past, present, or future—remember that the best is always before you. You can also pray the words of St. Patrick's famous breastplate prayer, which begins, "Christ, be with me."

Supplication: Jesus, whatever failures are behind me, keep your faithfulness before me; and whatever darkness lies within me, keep shining the light of your love upon me—and through me. Come, Holy Spirit. Amen.

6

True Faith Is a Costly Freedom

"You are worthy, O Lord … to receive glory and honor. …
For you created all things, and they exist because you
created what you pleased."

Revelation 4:11 NLT

God has been described as the hound of heaven, as one who chases us down with grace and runs after us with love. And truly, he is a God after our own hearts. "For God so loved the world, that he gave his only Son, that whoever believes in him should not perish but have eternal life" (John 3:16 ESV). So let us not forget that we are both extravagantly and irrevocably loved. But let us also remember that we too are to become people after God's own heart.

God pursues us so that he can know us, not simply so that we can know him. In fact, the extent to which we experience God matters less than the extent to which God experiences us. For the primary purpose of this life is to be known by God, just as the reward in the next is to know God (John 17:3). That is why, "Not everyone who says to [Jesus], 'Lord, Lord,' will enter the kingdom of heaven" (Matthew 7:21 ESV). Instead, it's those whom Jesus knows, and not necessarily those who know Jesus, who eventually—eternally—get to become as familiar with God as God has been familiar with them. "Now I know in part," as Paul said, "then I shall know fully, even as I am fully known" (1 Corinthians 13:12).

The principal purpose behind every personal relationship with God is not necessarily to feel loved by God, but to make God feel loved. This should not surprise us, however, because Jesus told us to, "Love the Lord your God with all your heart and with all your soul and with all your mind" (Matthew 22:37). Nor should it surprise us that what we do impacts how God feels, since the Bible contains ample evidence to that end.

But let us not think that we are doing more for God than God has done for us. For we love by God's love and we live by God's life. Indeed, we shall never live for God as God has lived—and died—for us; because, as the Bible says, "This is love: not that we loved God, but that he loved us and sent his Son as an atoning sacrifice for our sins" (1 John 4:10).

There is a certain liberty knowing that we can live such lives—by grace, through faith, and in love—as to make our Maker feel happy enough to smile and even weep. It's also encouraging to know that if we feel far from God, our faithfulness—however faltering—can allow God to feel closer to us. But this liberty is a costly freedom, since we cannot be free to love selflessly until we have been freed from living selfishly.

But we were born to be so free, because true life consists both in being loved and in loving with all of one's being. So let us pray for such a love—that we should become so loving—so that we can say with Paul, "It is no longer I who live, but Christ who lives in me" (Galatians 2:20 ESV).

Application: Create or find an inspirational reminder, such as a poem, picture, song, or Scripture, which will help you to remember that God loves you and that you are to love God.

Supplication: Lord, as much I should like to feel your love for me, help me to love you in such a manner that you will surely feel the love from me. Come, Holy Spirit. Amen.

7

Faith Speaks through Prayer

"The LORD will fight for you,
and you have only to be silent."

Exodus 14:14 ESV

If love is the life of faith, surely prayer is its language. For there is nothing so essential to faith as prayer, since faith is essentially a relationship, not merely a belief. To not pray to God—whom we love and who loves us so much more—is like children not talking to their parents or a spouse who remains silent at the dinner table.

Prayer is the language of faith, but it is nevertheless spoken with syllables of sound as well as silence. For prayer consists of things both said and unsaid, because love doesn't necessarily need to talk in order to communicate. In fact, there is both serenity and reassurance in the stillness of silence, because we don't have to fear the dreaded sound of a Zeus-like thunderbolt.

Nor do we have to fear that the distance between us will ultimately divide us. For just as there is a physical phenomenon called quantum entanglement, which as Marilynne Robinson explains, means that "particles that are 'entangled,' however distant from one another, undergo the same changes simultaneously,"[1] so there is a similar phenomenon that occurs during prayerful silence, when the Spirit that entangles our hearts with the heart of God shares a simultaneous love that no longer needs to be declared. It is the kind of love that can abide without having to confide, which can be enjoyed without silence being destroyed. For it's a moment when nothing has to be said and nothing needs to be done; it's the moment we see that love is what binds us together.

There are moments of silence, however, when our hushed serenity is supplanted by muted anxiety. It can stem from a fear—common in relationships—that when there is nothing left to say, there is no reason left to stay. It's based on the concern that a communication of words, rather than a communion of love, was the thing keeping us together. But that is not the case with God, because the basis of God's love for us is not how lovable we are—or even how much we love God—but instead is based on the fact that "God is love" (1 John 4:8).

Love is what holds us together in silence, but it is also what allows us to accept God's absence, which can seem like the ultimate silence. For the presence of God—the kind we feel—blows like a wind wherever it wishes. But "you who love Him," as Thomas Merton wrote, "must love Him as arriving from where you do not know and going where you do not know. ... Otherwise you do not respect His liberty to come and go as He pleases."[2] But such love still requires prayer—since prayer is precisely how we wait upon the Lord. Indeed, without prayer, there would be no substance behind the silence.

Application: Make yourself comfortable wherever you want, whether it's by the fire, in the bath, or on a walk. Take whatever you need to not fidget, such as a cup of tea, a glass of scotch, or a pencil and paper. And then rest in the silence of your situation, allowing your thoughts, and God's presence, the liberty to come and go as they please.

Supplication: Heavenly Father, I long to embrace both you and everything about you, but in the meantime, please help me with embracing both your occasional absence and your ostensible silence (along with my own silence too). Come, Holy Spirit. Amen.

8

Further,
My God, from Thee

And he went away and began to proclaim ...
how much Jesus had done for him,
and everyone marveled.

Mark 5:20 ESV

Between the commencement of spring and its consummation, there can be a season of contradiction—like cold snaps instead of crocuses, hail rather than hydrangeas, and deadwood not daffodils. But once the vernal equinox has occurred, we can be sure that spring has started, because every day thereafter the light lasts longer and the darkness grows shorter. Likewise, in the spiritual season of spring, there is a similar equinoctial shift that occurs. For just as we come to expect more of the sun in spring, so we also begin to expect more from the Son—from Jesus Christ.

Those who have given themselves to God hope that God

will give himself back to them. For there is a longing in our hearts to enter into "a further union, a deeper communion."[1] It is a yearning that goes beyond friendship and is even more intimate than marriage; it's the simple but singular desire for God himself. And this desire represents both our deepest and highest aspiration, because there is nothing more sincere than the genuine desire to be with God.

There was a man who was once tormented by a legion of demons until Jesus healed him. This man then longed to remain close to Jesus, so much so that he begged to go with him. Jesus, however, said no. Jesus told him, "Go home to your people and tell them how much the Lord has done for you" (Mark 5:19). But is it not sad that when this man tried to draw closer, Jesus drew further away? Is it not upsetting that it sometimes feels like we're also being dismissed—pushed away rather than pulled nearer?

Fortunately, the man in the story soon discovered that as good as it is to love God's presence, it is even greater to love God—present or absent. For such love enables us to come when God says come but also to go when (and where) God says go. It emboldens us to endure both the darkest nights of the soul and the bleakest days of the world. For so long as we trust that we're secure in God's heart, God will be secure in our hearts.

Besides, it's only when we learn to value personal obedience over spiritual experience that we become closer with Christ. Because, as Jesus said, "Whoever has my commandments and keeps them is the one who loves me … and I too will love them and show myself to them" (John 14:21).

Application: The next time you feel spiritually lonely, try writing a letter to yourself from the perspective of God, explaining how much you are loved as well as how this period of apparent isolation could actually be used for your benefit.

Supplication: God, if I love you enough to go where you go and to do what you do, help me to love you enough to also go where you do not seem to be and to do everything that you have already asked of me. Come, Holy Spirit. Amen.

9

Healthy Habits, Part 1

Whoever works his land
will have plenty of bread.

Proverbs 12:11 ESV

S pring is comprised of two opposing seasons: work and play—or more accurately, application and appreciation. For in the latter season, we can do things like relax and recline while picnicking in the park. But in the former season, we are busy applying ourselves in cleaning and cleansing, tilling and toiling, planting and sowing.

Likewise, when our faith (re)commences in spring, the season has elements of both serene appreciation and strenuous application. There are the obvious joys of grace working wonders and prayers being answered. But the very fact that we're born again means that we must learn how to live anew—new patterns, different choices, and healthier habits. To this end, Paul wrote, "put off your old self, which … is corrupt … and put on the new self … in true righteousness and holiness" (Ephesians 4:22–24 ESV).

It's said that manners maketh man. But it could also be said that habits maintaineth humans, because how we live our lives becomes the only lives that we live. It is imperative, therefore, that we give it all we've got—with all the grace we're given—to develop habits that help rather than hinder us. "Sow righteousness for yourselves," as Hosea said, and "reap the fruit of unfailing love" (Hosea 10:12).

Thomas à Kempis once wrote that if only we "eradicated one vice a year we should soon become perfect." Alas, he observed, "It is difficult to give up old habits and still more difficult to go against one's will."[1] But it is only difficult, not impossible. For a bad habit becomes its own punishment, just as Ovid said, "A virtue is its own reward."[2] So the faster we can fathom the price of vice and the value of virtue, the sooner we can screw our courage to the sticking place and resolve to become who we were meant to be yesterday but were delaying to be until tomorrow.

Paul said, "I have the desire to do what is right, but not the ability to carry it out" (Romans 7:18 ESV). This is because it takes grace, not greatness, to become totally transformed. That is not to say, however, that since grace does everything, we should do nothing. To the contrary, we have to do all that we can before we'll realize just how little we can do. In fact, we should be pouring ourselves out—all we are and all we can offer—because, as Thomas à Kempis said, "God bestows His blessings where He finds vessels that are empty [enough] to receive them."[3]

Application: Identify one bad habit that you can replace with a better one. Review your progress weekly.

Supplication: Lord, help me to remember that your grace does not do everything *for* me, but rather everything *with* me. Please continue to accompany me, therefore, in my every endeavor to become a better, healthier, and more wholesome human being. Come, Holy Spirit. Amen.

10

Healthy Habits, Part 2

Train up a child in the way
he should go.

Proverbs 22:6 ESV

John Wesley said, "Do all the good you can. By all the means you can. In all the ways you can … to all the people you can."[1] Indeed, let us always look to the good of others, but let us not overlook ourselves. For goodness without requires goodness within—as Jesus said, "A good man brings good things out of the good stored up in his heart" (Luke 6:45).

Naturally, such goodness is beyond us unless it's supernaturally within us. But it still remains our choice to work with this grace or against it. In fact, it's a decision that we're constantly making, because whoever we're becoming is being shaped by whatever we're doing. So let us consider the following habits, keeping in mind that "God is working in you, giving you the desire and power to do what pleases him" (Philippians 2:13 NLT).

The Habit of Thankfulness. Give thanks for whatever is good, whenever it's warranted, to whomever it's due—thereby adding even more to be thankful about, because "gratitude," as Cicero said, "is not only the greatest of virtues, it's the parent of all the rest."[2] For gratitude is a debt that loves to be repaid, with interest, and the more we give thanks, the more thankful we become.

The Habit of Journaling. God is not absent so much as we are absent-minded. For we receive various consolations, intimations, and communications, but they're forgotten over the span of a lifetime. Hence the common refrain, "Remember ... O Israel, you will not be forgotten by [God]" (Isaiah 44:21 ESV). To that end, we should keep a written record regarding our ongoing relationship with the Lord. Otherwise we run the risk of being like "someone who looks at his face in a mirror and ... goes away and immediately forgets what he looks like" (James 1:23–24).

The Habit of Rising Early. The obvious reason for rising early is to pray more effectively. This is what Jesus did for seclusion and concentration. But the less obvious reason for waking up early is that it's enjoyable. As the psalmist said, "Joy cometh in the morning" (Psalm 30:5 KJV). In fact, the earlier, the more joyful, because the world is exactly the way that we should be when dawn goes down to day: serene yet spirited. Indeed, whoever is voluntarily awake will invariably discover life at its happiest and healthiest, its most productive and profound. For all evil tends to be asleep by four, while joy and beauty are both awake by five—which is why we should be up no later than six.

Application: Pick one of the three suggested habits and practice it every day for two consecutive weeks.

Supplication: Jesus, as I adore your goodness, might I also aspire to be good. Come, Holy Spirit. Amen.

Healthy Habits, Part 3

Break up your fallow ground,
for it is time to seek the LORD.

Hosea 10:12 ESV

The spiritual disciplines are formal practices that effect
profound change—opening the mind, the body, and the
soul to God. Yet these disciplines can elicit admiration and
aversion in almost equal measure. For those who are free-
spirited and unregimented often dislike the spiritual disciplines because practices like fasting and confession can feel
too structured and insincere. While others can find great value
in spiritual disciplines like study and service because they
help us to develop self-control—perhaps even soul-control.

To the free-spirited, let it be said that authenticity is
admirable—so long as it is arduous. For a relationship with
God can be like other relationships. It sometimes requires
us to do things that we do not relish in order to preserve the
thing that we cherish—but love would always have us try,

and true love would have us try hard. So too, for the spiritually austere, while discipline is commendable, it must not become commanding. The spiritual disciplines can cooperate with the Spirit, but they can't commandeer it. Nor are they godly means to guaranteed ends, regardless of whether we're searching for saintly beatitude, moral rectitude, or financial plenitude. For no amount of discipline can transform our desires into God's duty.

The spiritual disciplines, which vary from meditation and study to submission and worship, are best undertaken not to experience God, but for God to experience us. For as much as we desire to abide in God, God desires to abide in us even more. "I stand at the door and knock," Jesus said, "If anyone ... opens the door, I will come in" (Revelation 3:20 ESV). Disciplines such as prayer and simplicity, therefore, are like doors we create into the houses of our hearts—opening ourselves to God.

Spiritual disciplines are also gifts that we can give to God. Fasting, for instance, can become the gift of gratitude, because a day without bread teaches us to be grateful for our daily bread. So too, solitude can impart the gift of undivided attention, because it teaches us how divided our lives have become. But that is not to say that more discipline is always more desirable—as though fanaticism could be synonymous with fidelity.

It is both saner and safer to be like Simon Peter, who fell asleep in prayer and thought about lunch while meditating, than like Simon Stylites, who lived atop a pillar for thirty-seven years to please the Lord. The disciplines, after all, are meant to vivify life, not vilify it, and to open us up to God, not to close us off to people. For it is not God's intention that we use the spiritual disciplines to leave this world behind, but to create sufficient space—in our homes and in our hearts, in our leisure and in our work life—to welcome God back into it.

Application: Examine your own usage of the spiritual disciplines, paying particular attention to the extent to which they are underdeveloped or overemployed.

Supplication: Lord, I want to be crazy about you but not crazy, to be zealous but not a zealot, to be pure but not a prude, and to be faithful but not fanatical. Walk with me, I pray, along this path of modest but meaningful devotion. Come, Holy Spirit. Amen.

12

God Give Me

"If you ask me anything in my name,
I will do it."

John 14:14 ESV

Jesus, help me
To pray with total clarity,
To see my own depravity,
To love with all sincerity,
And celebrate your verity.

Grant me
Faith for looking forward,
Grace for peering upward,
Trust to not go backward,
Hope to move heavenward.

Let my
Soul take flight,
To that great height,
Where there is no fight,
Since we love without sight.

Even if my only experience,
Is to render my existence,
Upward in persistence,
With true insistence,
To you.

Spare me
Not from the refiner's fire,
Where nothing's to desire,
Save what shall transpire:
The faith that's now afire.

Jesus, make me
A man for your own heart,
As I wasn't from the start;
So shape me part by part,
In this gracious, artless art.

Amen.

Application: Pray for the courage to triumph in your
trials, to overcome all obstacles, and to be ever faithful no

matter your feelings or fears. For inspiration, watch the six-time Academy Award-winning film about Sir Thomas More, *A Man for All Seasons*.

Supplication: Jesus, please guide me in all the ways that I should give myself to you, starting with the simple desire to actually do so. Come, Holy Spirit. Amen.

13

The Whirlwind, Part 1

If your law had not been my delight,
I would have perished in my affliction.

Psalm 119:92 ESV

One could easily mistake spring for a season of simple beauty and sublime tranquility—but it is as violent as it is vernal. "Nature," as Tennyson said, "is red, in tooth and claw."[1] It can be hard as hail and fearsome as a flood. It can wage a war of all against all, even upon itself. For the ferocity of a whirlwind—like a dust devil or a fire whirl, a tornado or a waterspout—can strip from the branch or scorch from the earth every other sign and symbol of spring.

Just as tornadoes have occurred on every continent except one, so they can occur in almost every stage and sphere of life. They may not have a two-mile diameter or wind speeds of three hundred miles per hour, but the whirlwinds we face—like inexplicable suffering, incurable disease, inconsolable loss, or intolerable trials—can be no less devastating.

Nor are they any less severe or infrequent if we happen to be enjoying a spring in our faith or a full-scale springtime in our spiritual lives. For the faith we have is what gets us through hardships; it does not necessarily get us out of them.

Faith is better suited to silencing the storms inside us, rather than unwinding the whirlwinds outside us. By all means, let's have faith enough to be healed or restored, but let us also have enough faith to not need healing or restoration. Indeed, we should have sufficient faith so God alone might suffice—so God can be our all in all.

Faith did not spare Joseph from prison, Job from sickness, or John from doubt. Faith did not even save them from death, because the fact remains, as Joseph de Maistre observed, "even the most moral man must die."[2] Instead, faith saved them from themselves—from the human tendency to mistake our desperation for God's desertion. It taught them to find grace in the middle of the gale and stillness at the center of the storm.

Yet the faith of these men never became a muzzle that silenced them, but was like a mouthpiece that spoke for them. Faith gave them the courage to ask for help in calamity, and the audacity to wait for it in adversity. It even gave them the humility to accept from God both the treasured yes and the dreaded no—not always with serenity but certainly with sincerity. For God is always willing to give—if we desire the grace to receive—the kind of faith that can trust beyond time, that can mature beyond mortality, that can enjoy health beyond healing, and that can find the life that's beyond living.

Application: Contemplate a reassuring passage from Scripture (for example, Matthew 11:28; Psalm 116:1–2; or Proverbs 3:5–6) while listening to Thomas Tallis' *Spem in alium*.

Supplication: Lord, I have faith, but sometimes things just fall apart; and I have hope, but occasionally everything looks a little hopeless. In such times, I pray that I might nevertheless have you, and that you might also have me. Come, Holy Spirit. Amen.

14

The Whirlwind, Part 2

Again Jesus said, "Simon … do you love me?"
John 21:16

When we are caught in the crosswinds of crisis and catastrophe, or disappointment and disorientation, we quickly look to Christ for comfort. Then—and sometimes only then—we take literally the words, "Come to me, all you who are weary and burdened, and I will give you rest" (Matthew 11:28). So we come with eyes of faith and a heart of hope, imploring the love that died for us to also live for us—that if not cured, we shall at least be cared for, and that even if we're lonely, we'll at least know we're not alone.

Jesus, although divine, was just as human as we are. Like us, he desired solidarity in sorrow and fatherly love during unfathomable affliction. Like us, he knew the pleasure of a burden shared, which is a burden halved, and the pain of a burden borne alone, which is a burden doubled. But unlike us, Jesus experienced the true agony of being alone—which is why he prayed, "My God, my God, why have you forsaken me?" (Matthew 27:46 ESV). Even more unlike us, as desirous as Jesus was for heaven's help, he desired even more to give heaven help—hence the prayer, "Not my will, but yours, be done" (Luke 22:42 ESV). For these were not the words of solemn service or stoic duty, but the tender realization of what a real relationship between God and us is meant to look like.

There is a God-shaped hole in every soul, which only God can fill—and a human-sized space within the heart of God, into which only we can fit. This void within us is involuntary, but the space within God is voluntary—it's there by volition and filled by volunteers. It is the purpose of our lives, therefore, to fill another life with love. In fact, "We have no other reason for being," Thomas Merton wrote, "except to be loved by him ... and to love him in return."[1] Naturally, though, we might wonder why it should be our lot in life to make an infinite and omnipotent deity feel loved, but if we really have to ask this question, then our love is in fact still questionable.

In the agony of life, we can still give the ecstasy of love. So when life has us down on our knees, let's stay on them, choosing to love in an unlovable situation. For that is when our faith is finally forged. That is when God gets to feel closer to us, regardless of how close we feel to God. As Paul said, "Whoever loves God is known by God" (1 Corinthians 8:3).

That does not mean, however, that should God get to know us better, we shall get to know him that much more (at least for now). In fact, we might still be crying, "My God, my God, why have you abandoned me?" But one day we shall hear God's grateful reply, "My child, my child, thank you for not abandoning me."

Application: To find comfort and encouragement in the dark days of faith, listen by candlelight to Rachmaninoff's *All-Night Vigil* (commonly translated as vespers).

Supplication: Lord, whatever the darkness is without, let there always be a light within—that however little I can see you, love shall allow you to see that much more of me. Come, Holy Spirit. Amen.

15

Praying with Faith

> "But you, take courage! Do not let your
> hands be weak, for your work shall be rewarded."
>
> *2 Chronicles 15:7* ESV

It takes great faith to genuinely pray for the lost to be found, the harmed to be healed, wrongs to be put right, and the world to wake up. But it takes even more faith to continue praying for such things with both unflagging faith and undimmed enthusiasm, not just once or twice but a thousand times over. For is it not the very definition of faith to keep praying the same thing, with the same hope, to the same God, the same every day, while arriving at the same unfulfilled outcome, without succumbing to the sensible conclusion that we're praying in vain and quite probably courting the insane?

Praying for something we know is right can sometimes feel quite wrong, if only because answered prayer can take so long. But the Bible would have us persevere—just as Abraham and Joseph did—because faith needs to thrive, not only by tackling the impossible, but also by persevering through the impossibly repetitive. Indeed, that was the message Jesus wanted to share with his disciples when he told them a certain parable: "to show them that they should always pray and not give up" (Luke 18:1). For in that parable a widow is refused justice until by dogged persistence she gets the judge to render her the correct verdict. As Jesus then remarked, if even an unjust judge was swayed by such steadfast insistence, "will not God, [who is truly just] bring about justice for his chosen ones, who cry out to him day and night?" (Luke 18:7).

It takes great faith to endure what's dangerous, but just as much to remain ardent when things are tedious and dull. It's imperative, therefore, that we cultivate a spirit of prayer that—far from being able to pray all night—prays night and day for an entire lifetime. But we also need faith—not just to wait for an answer to our own prayers but also to answer God's prayers. For God does pray—through the intercession of Jesus and the assistance of the Spirit—both in a general sense, but also for specific things that need to be done, but that nobody might want to do.

Some of these are simple things, like inviting recently arrived immigrants to dinner or donating more charitably to your local church; but others are more substantial, like selling your second home in order to give another family their first, leaving a good job to become a missionary far from home, or adopting a disabled or unwanted child.

The hardest part of prayer, requiring the largest amount of faith, is seldom getting what we want, but hearing and giving to God what he wants. Yet that's the most important step in spiritual progress and the greatest advance we can attain in prayer. Because we are told, "If we ask anything according to [God's] will, he hears us" (1 John 5:14).

Application: Go on a two-day prayer retreat. On the first day, pray with dogged perseverance about something that you truly desire. On the second day, pray with just as much insistence that God should have whatever he desires. If it is not feasible to go away for two days, follow a similar or shortened format at home on a weekend or on a walk.

Supplication: Lord, as daring as it is to pray for what I want, might I dare even more to pray for whatever you desire. Come, Holy Spirit. Amen.

16

Keeping Faith with the Faithful

"I pray that they will all be one,
just as you and I are one."

John 17:21 NLT

We stand as individuals before God, but not as isolated individuals. For the degree to which we're invited to be sons and daughters of God, is the same degree we're called to become brothers and sisters to one another. We're called to keep faith with the faithful, to be members of the church.

The church is undoubtedly a highly dysfunctional family, living in different homes, under different surnames, with different opinions of each other. But we are one family—far from united by our love for one another—but united by God's love for us, which creates a communion of love between us, assisted by fellowship in the Holy Spirit. It's a fellowship we're all invited to join, though few choose to enter.

It is much simpler to be a Christian than a churchgoer, since it is much easier to focus on our voluntary love for God, rather than be forced into what feels like an involuntary love for one another. But that is one of the primary advantages of going to church, because we are forced into a community of love rather than isolated in a camaraderie of like. For if it was up to us, we'd probably only love those we like, whereas God would have us love all those he loves.

This means, within the metaphor of the church body, that we can't dismiss each other. The learned can't say to the ignorant, "We don't need you," nor can the militant say to the mild, "We don't acknowledge you," anymore than, "The eye cannot say to the hand, 'I don't need you!'" (1 Corinthians 12:21). For a body is made from many parts—some of which are far from dignified—so we must show kindness even to those we like the least or disagree with the most (as even those resembling an anus still have a place in the body). After all, Paul said, "The parts that are unpresentable are [to be] treated with special modesty. ... [For] you are the body of Christ, and each of you is a part of it" (1 Corinthians 12:23–27).

To be sure, there are times when a lack of common belief is cause for a cancellation of communion, but such times are also an occasion for uncommon love. Because Jesus said we must be known by our love—for our coreligionists, neighbors, and even our enemies. So let us extend to each other goodwill and good works, wise words and compassionate prayers. For the profit we do posterity by guarding our doctrinal truths might be of little benefit to us, because as Thomas à Kempis wrote, "If [we] know the whole Bible by heart, and all the teachings of the [theologians], what good would that be [to us] without the grace and love of God?"[1]

Application: It is easier to connect with people in church if we are also connected to them outside church. So organize a social event for you and a few people from your faith community.

Supplication: Jesus, as you are to me, may I be to others. That the way I am welcomed, I shall welcome; the way I am forgiven, I shall forgive; and the way I am loved, I shall love. Come, Holy Spirit. Amen.

17

No Pain, No Gain

Do not arouse … love until it so desires.

Song of Solomon 2:7

Mahatma Gandhi once said that the weak couldn't forgive since it took great strength to be forgiving. And there is certainly some truth in this, because forgiveness requires more from the forgiver than the forgiven. For the injured party must take pains to be humble and not haughty, as well as genuine rather than begrudging. So it's not hard to imagine Peter's dismay once he had asked Jesus, "Lord, how many times shall I forgive my brother or sister who sins against me? Up to seven times?" to which Jesus answered, "I tell you, not seven times, but seventy-seven times" (Matthew 18:21–22).

This much clemency goes beyond common sense. Yet it's entirely possible that the reason for all this forgiving has less to do with the quantity of our mistakes and more to do with the mistaken quality of our forgiveness. For the finality of our forgiveness is rarely one and done. Instead, it's often one and undone, because as hard as it is to forgive, it's even harder to remain forgiving. This is not necessarily due to a lack of love. In fact, it sometimes seems like the more effort we put into providing a loving pardon, the longer the process of forgiving and forgetting can become.

The pain of betrayal is not easily remedied, because the past is no respecter of the present, since old pains continually find new ways of being felt. It's often the case, however, that we try to bandage our wounds before we've actually disinfected them, and progress on to love before we've processed through pain. Naturally, while we mustn't try to add grief to our grievances or listlessness to our love, we must have faith enough to probe our pain before we can proceed with our piety. This is because forgiveness is like an anchor. It has to reach rock bottom before it can be effective. We need to know just how much we've been hurt before we can know just how much to forgive.

The Bible tells us not to hate; it does not say that we do not hate. Likewise, we're also told to love our enemies, not that we don't have any. In order to love more earnestly, therefore, we must look into ourselves more honestly. That is not to say we'll like what we see, or that we should validate what we find. Indeed, the vicious or vengeful tone in some of the Psalms is far from virtuous. Yet their honesty is what makes them helpful. They remind us that if we try to hide our darkness from

God, we shall also hide our light from others, because pain has to be confessed before it can be addressed. So until we recognize our hate, we'll always remain hateful; until we see that we have enemies, we can't love our enemies as we should; and so long as we keep from ourselves who we really are, we won't become the people we're really meant to be.

Application: Examine a past or present pain and grant yourself the liberty to feel what you really felt and to think what you actually thought. Then pray for the grace to forgive as you have been forgiven.

Supplication: Jesus, please walk with me through my pain, rather than around it. Let me see how I've been hurt—and how I've been hurting others—so I'll know what to forgive and how much I also need forgiveness. Come, Holy Spirit. Amen.

18

To Grow or Not to Grow?

"This is to my Father's glory, that you bear much fruit,
showing yourselves to be my disciples."

John 15:8

Bernard of Clairvaux once said, "We find something more in the woods than in books."[1] Indeed, we find ourselves—our potential—personified in the charm of a cherry tree, in the simplicity of a pine, and in the grandeur of a great oak. For these characteristics and others correspond with the character we would like to have—that we shall have—since the Bible does say, "they will be like a tree planted by the water" (Jeremiah 17:8).

That doesn't mean, however, that the more we grow like trees, the more we'll resemble the trees we like. For trees don't always grow as they should. Instead, they can grow sideways and in odd ways, like aspens bent by a late-spring snowfall and fir trees forked by lightning. But these trees are still real trees, because what they grow matters more than how they grow. "The tree," Jesus said, "is known by its fruit" (Matthew 12:33 ESV).

The mark of a good life is not the degree to which it resembles a beautiful tree—because serenity, solidity, and sublimity are not realistic measurements—but the extent to which one's life can create more life, like grapes on a vine and berries on a bush. As the Bible says, "A good life is [like] a fruit-bearing tree" (Proverbs 11:30 MSG). Thus it does not matter how misshapen our lives are; so long as we have faith we have life, because grace "never fails to bear fruit" (Jeremiah 17:8). Indeed, grace creates an abundant harvest, because the fruit of the Spirit ranges from love and joy to peace and patience.

God cares more about the fruit than the tree, while we often care more about the tree than the fruit. In fact, we'd rather bear little fruit as a great tree than bear great fruit as a little tree—or we would at least prefer to be a straight tree before producing shapely fruit: gaining before giving, and served before serving. But grandness cannot be had without goodness, because only "the fruit of the righteous is a tree of life" (Proverbs 11:30).

So we must decide between having the humility to accept whatever growth can be had—so often in a soil that's not our choosing, in a direction that's not our deciding, and in a manner that's not our making—or laboring under the vain but wonderful delusion that we can become whoever we wish, whenever we want, and however we choose.

But that isn't to say that we won't emerge in time (or eternity) as something beautiful, sizable, and whole. "The righteous," after all, "will flourish like a palm tree, they grow like a cedar of Lebanon" (Psalm 92:12). Only righteousness itself requires the meekness to begin as the little tree, the misshapen tree—the cross-shaped tree.

Application: As a living analogy, plant a tree and watch it gradually grow and mature.

Supplication: Thank you, God, that you have planted my life in time and that you delight as you watch it slowly growing into eternity. Come, Holy Spirit. Amen.

19

Full-Time Faithfulness

I keep my eyes always on the LORD.

Psalm 16:8

The Bible encourages us to always pray, rejoice, meditate, and do good. But this can be discouraging for those not living or working in a monastery or church, because a life of such mysticism can look like a lack of professionalism—that if we are always praying, we are never working. But many of those who strove to live such lives in the Bible were also professionals, tradesmen, administrators, and the like.

God knows that we must work, because God invented working. He also encourages us to seek assistance in our profession (Psalm 90:7), to find satisfaction and remuneration (Proverbs 14), and to "work willingly at whatever you do, as though you were working for the Lord rather than for people" (Colossians 3:23 NLT). So when we are told to be ever faithful—even at work—that doesn't mean we should do less work. It simply means that the life within us—the Holy

Spirit—should become integrated in the outward life of our daily routines.

The best way to be always praying and always rejoicing while at work is to have momentary but meaningful times that are scheduled for such activities throughout the day. That might be a three-minute prayer pause at midmorning, a short psalm session at noon, and four minutes in the afternoon listening to a worship song. But it doesn't matter what or when it is, so much as the fact that we are prioritizing in tangible ways the most important but intangible priority in our life. Granted, some of us have hectic and high-powered jobs, with unexpected demands and tight deadlines, but if we cannot spare a few minutes for God, why should God—save for the sake of Jesus Christ—spare for us even a moment's notice?

The impact that a few minutes each working day can have might seem minor, but it contributes to our growth no less than daily watering contributes to the growth of a plant. And the difference it makes, while imperceptible from day to day, can be perceived over time, because it's the difference between flourishing and perishing.

It should be noted, however, that brief intervals for devotion are not well suited to squeezing in life-changing spiritual experiences, metaphysical epiphanies, or emotional ecstasies. In fact, if we are trying to find God in these moments, there might be little to find. Instead, these quick but conscientious acts of prayer and worship are best suited for enabling God to find us. To find a heart he can inhabit, whether we realize we're being inhabited or not. For that is something God desires each and every day: a heart to call home, a friend to call his own, and a life that is always open to being known.

Application: Schedule a few reoccurring appointments throughout your day where you can quietly but concretely offer yourself back to God.

Supplication: Lord, as you have not forgotten me, might I not forget you. So I give to you—by the very grace you have given me—some of the scarcest and most sacred gifts that I have to offer, which are my time and attention. Come, Holy Spirit. Amen.

20

Faith from a Book

"I will put my law in their minds
and write it on their hearts."

Jeremiah 31:33

To have faith in the power of faith, without due regard for what exactly we have faith in, is like believing in progress for the sake of progress without knowing to what end we're progressing. As Leo Tolstoy observed, "[This is] like a person who is in a boat being carried along by the wind and waves and who when asked the most important and vital question, 'Where should I steer?' avoids answering by saying, 'We are being carried somewhere.'"[1]

We do not have faith in faith itself, but faith in our Father—in God himself. Nor do we believe in a father of our own projection, but in one made apprehensible in time by Jesus and also comprehensible through time by the Bible. Indeed, the Bible is our surest guide to what we need to know about God—even though it doesn't contain all we can or should like to know—because it preserves for all posterity the salutary and saving words, deeds, and desires of God.

John Locke rightly stated, "The Bible is one of the greatest blessings bestowed by God."[2] But the Bible is a book that becomes a blessing not necessarily when it is read, but when it is believed. In fact, there is little to its lyricism, or merit in its morals, or any point to its plot save for the fact that there is truth in its telling. Indeed, that there is truth worth hearing. For the Bible—though not itself the way, the truth, and the life—leads us to Jesus, who is very much the way, the truth, and the life.

There is nothing spiritually inspiring about reading a book that is inspired by the Spirit unless we're willing to have the words that we read written upon our hearts. For it is only when the Bible is written inside us that others can read the Bible through us—by reading our words, actions, and aspirations. So let's read the Bible as best we can, because we might be the only Bible that somebody else reads.

Indeed, we should study it intelligently, because every text has a context to know; and read it referentially, since the present has no monopoly on the past. Likewise, we should ponder it patiently, for as much as we want to hear what it has to say, we still have to wait long enough to let it speak; and consider it prayerfully, because just as it's in God that we live and move and have our being, so it's with God that we should do our reading. And lastly, we ought to read it deferentially, because the Bible is not just to be believed but also obeyed; and experientially, because its truths need to be lived as much as they need to be learned.

Application: Devise a reading plan that enables you to read from the Bible at least two chapters a day, every day of the year. To assist your effort, consider downloading or subscribing to Nicky Gumbel's Bible in One Year app/e-mail service.

Supplication: Jesus, please help me to read your word with the mind of a scholar, the heart of a believer, and the soul of a servant. Come, Holy Spirit. Amen.

21

Great Expectations

Nathanael said to [Jesus], "How do you know me?"

John 1:48 ESV

A rich young man once approached Jesus and asked him, "Good Teacher, what must I do to inherit eternal life?" (Mark 10:17 ESV). The young man's inquiry was sincere and earnest, but he was nevertheless disappointed when Jesus said, "You lack one thing: go, sell all that you have and give to the poor ... and come, follow me" (Mark 10:21 ESV). For the young man had come to Jesus with great but misguided expectations: intending to find goodness, not God; heavenly riches, not earthly poverty; and profound insights, not divine commands. So the man left, doubly dejected, aware that his possessions now possessed him, since he was only willing to love God with a lot of his heart, but not all of it.

The rich young man did nothing that we haven't done, because most of us love God with a lot of our heart but not quite with all of it. Like him, we're perhaps willing to give away much of what we possess—which is more than most—but we're nevertheless unwilling to imagine a scenario wherein we'd have to be dispossessed of everything. For we all have the capacity to love the gifts that God gives us as much or more than the gift that is God. The only difference between us is that the rich young man had the blessed misfortune to be asked directly whether he was willing to love the Maker above his money and the Savior before his security.

The benefits that God bestows do not always seem so beneficial to us. For the rich young man, losing his money seemed like he was losing his life. But he was offered the gift of detachment so that he could become more attached to God—or rather, so that God could become more attached within him. For this man was already treasured in Jesus' heart, only Jesus was not treasured in his heart. The gifts of God, therefore, though varied, are first of all intended not to enable us to dive deeper into God but to allow God to delve further into us. For this is the rationale of our religion and the reason behind our relationship: to let love open our hearts to God, just as God's heart is already open to us.

It is a false impression, however, to presume that the more we love God, the more we'll experience him. On the contrary, the more we love God, the more God experiences us. For this life is primarily about God knowing us, and the next about us knowing him. It is imperative, therefore, that we cultivate a heart that's open to Christ, because whatever we cannot allow God to give us will become a reason why we cannot give ourselves to God.

Application: Examine your heart in order to find something you would have great trouble giving up or giving away should God ask you to do so. Then pray, not necessarily for the opportunity to do this, but at least for the willingness to do so.

Supplication: God, regardless of whether I am obliged to give something away, grant me the willingness to give everything away. Embolden me, because the more I give for you, the more I am giving to you, and the less I have because of you, the less I have beside you. Come, Holy Spirit. Amen.

22

Faith and Finances

Give me neither poverty nor riches,
but give me only my daily bread.

Proverbs 30:8

Lord, regarding wealth please hear my prayer:
   Give me more than a little, lest I curse my life,
   For the lack of money is its own source of evil.
   But not so much that it becomes a curse on me,
   Since the love of money is not the love of thee.

But heart, on these moneyed thoughts do dwell:
   That if little I get, let it not be little that I give,
   Or a lot—be content—as much will have more.
   And remember, if rich, the wealthy are damned,
   Not for becoming rich, but for not giving richly.

And soul, on these thoughts of wealth, think well:
    Should I get some dollars, also get some sense:
    Recalling that I'm more than the money I earn,
    But less for the wealth that I selfishly withhold
    From heaven's cause and neighbors' true needs.

And mind, take heed, since for thee tolls this bell:
    The faithfulness of giving, is a faith that is living,
    And what I do with wealth, is then done with me:
    Because the spirit I give in, the Spirit gives to me,
    The measure I used with others: now used on me.

Application: There is a powerful link between our faith and our finances. To better understand this connection, read or watch Charles Dickens' *A Christmas Carol*.

Supplication: Lord, thank you that it is not wrong to like money, but do help me to remember that it is wrong to love money—save for the love of giving it away. Come, Holy Spirit. Amen.

23

Where's the Gratitude?

Give thanks to the LORD, for he is good.

Psalm 136:1

Spring is a perennial surprise, both seasonally and spiritually, because its wonders are as improbable as they are delightful. For it is nothing, if not unlikely, that bare and spindly branches should be able to produce verdant buds and fragrant blossoms. Nor is it anything short of astounding that the monochromatic shimmer of winter yields to the kaleidoscopic colors of spring. So too, in the springtime of the soul, there is something unexpected and astonishing about how we go from lost to found, faithless to faithful, vice to virtue, and mundane to miraculous.

Yet the further we progress into the heart of religion, the easier it becomes to regress within our very own hearts. For the more we advance in the faith—from follower to leader, learner to teacher, beneficiary to benefactor—the harder it is to remain humble. And the more virtuous we become—forbearing, generous, and self-controlled—the more tempted we are to mistake God's grace for our goodness. Indeed, the further we are from winter, the faster we forget whom to thank for spring.

Superficial growth comes from us, but supernatural growth comes from the Lord. To mature in a meaningful manner, we must remember the Lord, for it is he who gives us the power to grow. To this end, Paul wrote, "Give thanks in all circumstances, for this is God's will for you in Christ Jesus" (1 Thessalonians 5:18). Give thanks, as Paul said, because gratitude is what keeps the Lord's name upon our lips, before our minds, and within our hearts.

One of the beauties of gratitude is that it blesses the one who thanks as well as the one being thanked. For just as those who ask shall receive, so those who say thank you shall receive all the more (partly because gratitude is its own reward, but also on account of the fact that God enjoys giving to the grateful). Likewise, gratitude fulfills our fundamental longings to give credit where credit is due, and to know whom to give credit to.

In fact, not only does gratitude do us much good, but it's also the reason behind much of the good that we do. The reason for this being that "we love because [God] first loved us" (1 John 4:19). Indeed, we love out of gratitude because we're grateful for love. So let us give thanks to the Lord since "his love endures forever" (Psalm 118:1). But let's not just say thanks; let's live thankfully, because gratitude is not what we say, it's what we do.

Application: At the end of every day, write down in a journal at least three things for which you are grateful. In times of difficulty or aridity, return to these entries.

Supplication: Lord, grant to me the grace of a long gratitude, so that far from just saying thank you, I shall also live thankfully too. Come, Holy Spirit. Amen.

24

When You're Sixty-Four

When I became a man, I gave up childish ways.

1 Corinthians 13:11 ESV

In faith's first blossom, love also blooms. For when we encounter an infinite love, we feel infinitely loved; and nothing quickens our adoration like God's affection. In such a season it can seem both effortless and instinctual to love the Lord with boundless affection and attention, enrapture and intimacy, adoration and adherence.

There are times, later in life or further in faith, when the intensity of young love seems beyond the beckoning call of an older heart. In these moments we can feel unlovable or incapable of such love, as though true faith were behind us, because love is beyond us. Yet the heart still longs for what it lacks. As Mother Teresa reportedly said, "The hunger for love is more difficult to remove than the hunger for bread."

The desire to love again can be inseparable from the desire to feel loved again. But this can be a dangerous desire, because love must sometimes play the lover and not the beloved—to be selfless and not selfish. As William Blake wrote, love can either "seeketh itself not to please ... but for another gives its ease," or love can "seeketh only self to please ... [and] joy in another's loss of ease."[1]

Such as it is, the past is often beyond the reach of our present. We cannot, for instance, always love the Lord the way we once did, because we are no longer the people we once were. For one's life is like a series of lives woven together with the strand of a single soul. Who we became is not necessarily who we shall become, and the love we gave is not always the love we can give.

Love is best measured by constancy, not consistency—by what it can do, not what it can't do. So let's focus on the love that is before us, that leads beyond us—outward to our neighbors and upward to God. For one's life is only as large as their love. It does little good, therefore, to pine for the life that we had when our faith began, because faith itself is at its liveliest not when it's delightful but when it's most decisive.

The Bible says that love never ends, not that our love shall never change. Indeed, it's so changeable because we change how we feel all the time; one moment we're limitless, the next listless. Yet the mark of love is what it does, not how it feels. In fact, love is but the life of faith and faith the life of love, because love must always act in good faith, and faith should always act as though in love.

Application: Talk to someone who has been a believer for decades about the various ways in which their capacity to give and receive love has changed and matured.

Supplication: Lord, help me to measure my love, not just by what I desire but also what I do—and I pray that I do nothing except love you. Come, Holy Spirit. Amen.

25

Losing Faith, Part 1

Out of the depths I cry to you, O LORD!

Psalm 130:1 ESV

Faith is about dealing with doubt as much as it is about having a hope or maintaining a belief. For it besets both the young and old, faithful and faltering, mature and unwise with equal importunity. It even assails the seemingly redoubtable, like John the Baptist, whose own birth was miraculously foretold and who had received miraculous signs regarding Jesus. Yet even he had doubts in a dark and desperate hour, while locked away in Herod's dungeon. So we can rest assured if we're feeling doubtful. To doubt is to be amongst very devout company.

When in doubt, there are certain things we can do—not necessarily to avoid our doubting but to put to rest some of our fears about being doubtful. Because doubt is not something to be feared, so much as it's to be recognized and utilized—since doubt is not the absence of faith but rather the opportunity for it.

To begin, know that doubting something does not automatically disprove it, nor does it discredit the one who doubts. To be doubtful is not necessarily a sign of spiritual failure but rather a hallmark of being human. It's what C. S. Lewis called "the law of undulation."[1] For all life—whether theological or biological—has its highs and its lows.

Just as doubt doesn't devalue our faith, so it can also enrich it. For something powerful occurs when someone "looks round upon a universe from which every trace of [God] seems to have vanished, and asks why [they] have been forsaken, and still obeys."[2] In fact, such faith—however faithless one might feel—is worth many a miracle, since the soul must learn to love through faith and hope, which seldom occurs save in doubt, danger, and disappointment.

Doubt also reveals what routine conceals: that we're neither as abiding as we assumed, nor as courageous as we presumed. For it does not take much doubt to prove that our faith is fleeting and our convictions are unconvincing. But the value of doubt is nevertheless indispensable, because the clarity we can gain is indisputable. "Look at men in the midst of doubt," as Lucretius said, "and you will learn in his hour of adversity what he really is."[3] Look, because doubt shows us how hard it is to live as we were made to and to love as we were bade to. But look again, because grace can turn our weakness into greatness. "My grace is sufficient for you," Jesus said, "for my power is made perfect in weakness" (2 Corinthians 12:9). And then keep looking—however doubtfully—beyond ourselves and on to Jesus, because then we shall see that, as Paul said, "when I am weak, then I am strong" (2 Corinthians 12:10). Then we'll know that doubt can sometimes be our friend rather than always having to be our foe.

Application: Record a short voice memo about the ways in which doubt can be both normal and potentially helpful, then listen to it whenever you are feeling doubtful.

Supplication: God, thank you that your patience extends to those struggling with perseverance, and your grace encompasses those who are trying but also failing to love you. Please use my weakness as an occasion for your strength, helping me to see beyond the little faith that I have, to all the faithfulness that you have. Come, Holy Spirit. Amen.

26

Losing Faith, Part 2

"I do believe; help me overcome my unbelief!"
Mark 9:24

Doubt is not the failure of faith, but the occasion for it. Likewise, while doubt reveals the limitations of our faith, it also presents us with the opportunity to entrust ourselves into God's faithfulness. So let's explore how we can best understand, endure, and even be enriched by our doubt, since it's not something we can always avoid.

To begin, it helps to know that our doubts arise from conflicting desires as much as from criticizing dogmas. For human faith has to coordinate—and contend—with human nature, which combines our spirituality, rationality, emotionality, physicality, sexuality, and more. So a doubt is not necessarily driven by rational concerns or personal problems but drawn by desires that have the power to undermine our beliefs. As even Friedrich Nietzsche observed, "When a man tries earnestly to liberate his intellect, his passions and desires secretly hope to benefit from it also."[1] To confront our doubts, therefore, we should not just look at what we stand to lose but also at what our desires had hoped to gain.

As important as it is to combat our doubts, doubting should still be conducted as a fair fight. It should be undertaken with an open mind—asking hard questions, reading important critiques, and considering studied responses—because faith without thought is a thoughtless faith. Similarly, being doubtful requires a discerning eye—looking at all the facts and factors in both the hard places and dark spaces, because believing without seeing is just blind faith.

Doubt is also amplified when we feel alone. But we are not alone. The faith that we hold is held around the world. And it's been doubted before us and will be doubted after us. In fact, it's been doubted—but then believed—millions of times over, over thousands of years, by billions of people. So when in doubt, recall that we are not alone, and do not forget the passages and promises that have sustained hundreds of doubtful generations. Because as Jesus said, "Behold, I am with you always, to the end of the age" (Matthew 28:20 ESV).

If at the end of all our attempts at faithfulness, however, it seems as if doubt has won and faith has failed, know that all can still be well. For there is surely hope in the simple desire to still have faith, just as there is grace for those who truly want to want to have faith—because even that is a form of faithfulness. True, it's slight and miniscule, but it only takes faith the size of a mustard seed to move a mountain.

Application: Print and frame the passage, "I do believe; help me overcome my unbelief!" (Mark 9:24).

Supplication: Lord, when I'm doubtful I often don't know what to say to you. But I pray that you'll somehow hear these words: I love you, I need you, I miss you, and I want to believe in you. Come, Holy Spirit. Amen.

Signs Won't Save Us

"Why does this generation ask for a sign?
Truly I tell you, no sign will be given to it."

Mark 8:12

It's said that a faithless generation asked Jesus for signs, but if we are honest, many of the faithful would also like to receive a sign: a miracle, a vision, or some kind of wonder. And yet, no sign seems to come. So we could ask God, "Why not?" But God might reply, "The signs you desire will not in fact produce the faith I want."

God actually protects us from ourselves by not always giving us signs, because to do so would ingrain the wrong habits. For we prefer to grow our faith through shortcuts: desiring signs like a desperate athlete wanting steroids—for immediate growth and a quick victory. But it is always better to grow our faith the right way—the hard way—like athletes who train with discipline and dedication. For then our faith is forged through actual faithfulness.

Just as signs can be a dangerous shortcut for immature believers, so they can also have a deadening influence on the mature. For an overabundance of signs creates an over-dependence on them. It can create a situation wherein it takes a sign or a special word to get us to do anything, rather than us doing something because the Bible instructs to do so. Indeed, it interferes with the basic arithmetic of belief, because it removes from the equation our own trust and initiative. It means that God must wait upon us rather than us waiting upon God. But a sign is nothing more than a symbol; it's not a solution, and it cannot do the hard work of faith for us.

God withholds certain things from us because, far from blessing us, they might in fact break us. For a sign is no mere spectacle; it is a moment of profound decision wherein we have to respond to God—not just yea or nay, but whether we're all in or not. Which is one reason why God keeps so many miracles from us: lest we end up on the wrong side of one.

For what hope is there for a person who had eyes but chose not to see, or who was healed but never returned in thanks? As Jesus remarked, "Woe to you! ... Woe to you! ... For if the miracles that were performed in you were performed in Sodom, it would have remained to this day" (Matthew 11:21–23). So we're often kept in the dark—out of mercy and not malice—until that day when we'll no longer be so blinded by the light.

God desires our faith to have "confidence in what we hope for and assurance about what we do not see" (Hebrews 11:1). Such faith does not need to see signs, because this kind of faith can see with the eyes of love. For it longs to show God the signs of its own faithfulness, and not just to receive them. Just as it hopes to make God feel loved, not merely to feel loved by God. Granted, such faith might appear blind before others, but it simply apprehends what others have failed to comprehend: that our faith is a sign of God's own faithfulness.

Application: Pray for the opportunity to show God a sign of your faithfulness.

Supplication: Lord, as a lover longs to show their love, may my faith yearn to show its faithfulness—not for the sake of my holiness, but for your happiness. Come, Holy Spirit. Amen.

28

The Dark Forces

Do not be overcome by evil,
but overcome evil with good.

Romans 12:21

It is misleading to talk about God without mentioning the devil, or to speak of what is good without acknowledging evil. For evil is a reality that unsettles us daily—or it should. Granted, it's not socially correct or scientifically demonstrable to describe something as evil, but as the noted historian Leszek Kołakowski has observed, "The Devil is part of our experience. Our generation has seen enough for the message to be taken seriously."[1] Indeed, the dark forces that lurk behind the human experience must be taken seriously, because they contribute so much to our own trials and temptations.

It's all too easy to miss the mark when it comes to how we approach the problem of evil. As C. S. Lewis wrote, "There are two equal and opposite errors into which our race can fall about the devils. One is to disbelieve in their existence. The other is to believe, and to feel an excessive and unhealthy interest in them."[2] Indeed, to not believe in the agency of evil is to become unaware of the extent to which all our endeavors can become undermined and intertwined with deceitful and injurious outcomes. But too great an interest can lead some toward the occult, while in others—especially those who are religious—it can turn into suspicion, superstition, and fanaticism. In fact, the fear of evil has robbed the world of much good and turned many people into the very evil they revile.

The Bible does acknowledge that "your enemy the devil prowls around like a roaring lion looking for someone to devour" (1 Peter 5:8). But that same verse adds, "Be alert and of sober mind." Indeed, we should be sober minded, because we should lose something dear if we lost our common sense. For evil often rears its head precisely when we lose our own. So let's look to these simple but sound practices so that when temptations do arise, neither sin nor foolishness shall abound:

1) Quietly but forcefully employ the commanding name of Jesus.

2) Sing a psalm in your heart, repeating as necessary a poignant phrase like, "Come to my help, O God. Lord, hurry to my rescue."

3) Listen to music, as Saul did the harp, until the moment passes. For we can certainly blast a thing back to hell with Beethoven's Ninth Symphony!

4) The Bible says to run from temptation. But literally running, on a jog, can help ease the tension that comes from the temptations of the flesh.

5) Eat something low in sugar, high in protein, and nutritional, because willpower and self-control correlate with our body's glucose levels.[3]

6) Confide your temptations to someone trustworthy, because a burden shared is a burden halved.

7) Kneel somewhere private and pray for the help of the Holy Spirit.

8) Lastly, take courage and have faith. God can work all things for good, including our shortcomings and failures. For if God could not do that, then God could not do much—at least not with any of us.

Application: Create your own temptation toolkit that you can access whenever you feel enticed by the enemy.

Supplication: Lord, for every path that leads to you, there are thousands that run away from you. So I pray that you'll walk with me, while also teaching me how to walk with you. Come, Holy Spirit. Amen.

29

Caviar and the Cross

"The Son of Man
came eating and drinking."

Luke 7:34

Continents submerge, mountains erode, forests burn, and rivers run dry. These are but fleeting things, like all the other things of this world, including the world itself. As Robert Frost wrote, "Nature's first green is gold, / Her hardest hue to hold. / Her early leafs a flower; / But only so an hour … / So dawn goes down to day. / Nothing gold can stay."[1]

Indeed, nothing gold can stay, which is one reason why some people choose to stay away, segregating themselves from the transient charms of this world. In their minds, it's better to esteem the eternal over the temporal, because whatever's not infinite might be insidious, whatever's not timeless could be a temptation, and if something's not pure it's probably impure—like a metaphysical version of Murphy's Law.

There is another perspective, however, that does not measure the dignity of something by its duration, or by the cries of damnation. Instead, it takes delight in everything that's truly delightful, from marigolds and mountains to merlot and filet mignon, because matter is like manna from heaven: giving us strength for the body, sustenance for the mind, and stimulus for the soul. After all, it is, "by means of all created things, without exception, [that] the divine assails us, penetrates us and molds us."[2]

Furthermore, it's by means of matter that we can celebrate the fact that in saving our souls, God has not neglected our bodies. So, as Paul said, "Whether you eat or drink ... do all to the glory of God" (1 Corinthians 10:31 ESV). Indeed, we can be quite confident about doing so, as "there is nothing better ... than to eat and drink and be glad" (Ecclesiastes 8:15).

There is a balance, however, to be had between fasting and feasting. Virtue, after all, lives in the middle and vice at the extremes. To forgo what's good, in order to forbear what's bad, can definitely be taken too far—just as enjoyment can easily devolve into indulgence and extravagance.

It is with the spirit of self-control, therefore, that we should not keep for ourselves whatever should be kept from others. Nor should we selfishly give to ourselves something that cannot be selflessly given to another. And we should also take care lest our joy become another's woe, and our celebration someone else's scandal. For the mark of a good thing is the goodness that it bestows, which is why we can still be bold about the blessings of a banquet—because, as Jesus said, "When you give a banquet, invite the poor, the crippled, the lame, the blind, and [all of] you will be blessed" (Luke 14:13–14).

Application: Cook the dinner, uncork the wine, set the table, and invite all the unwanted to dine.

Supplication: Lord, help me to celebrate—with moderation but exaltation—the good things of creation, while also remembering to celebrate—without moderation and with adoration—the goodness of its great and wonderful creator. Come, Holy Spirit. Amen.

30

The Way of Wisdom

Get wisdom. Though it cost you all you have,
get understanding.

Proverbs 4:7

To read a book by someone like Michel de Montaigne or Thomas Browne can feel as if we're reading something that was written by wisdom itself. For it has the uncanny but exhilarating feeling that we're being told something we somehow knew, but we're still being taught more than we actually know. Sadly, however, life won't let us begin where these authors end, since agreeing with something wise does not make us someone who is wise. For there is an art to wisdom, and it consists as much in what we do as what we know.

It would be a mistake to think that since we know what we ate at a restaurant, we could easily make at home what we've just eaten. For it takes more than a recipe to become a chef, just as it requires more than wisdom to become wise. There is an art to both, and we must learn the art of living in order to live wisely. That isn't to say that reading wise books and talking to wise people is a poor attempt at solving this problem.

By all means, dust off the old dons and dames like John Ruskin and Julian of Norwich. But know, as Marcel Proust wrote, "While we would like them to provide us with answers ... all they are able to do is provide us with desires."[1] For the past can always teach us, but the present still has to learn anew—because every generation must discover for themselves how to order their loves, number their days, find their faith, and live their lives.

The beauty of wisdom is the way that it unfolds reality, unlocking new thoughts, which we can then explore like new rooms. But just as wisdom is what unlocks life's wonder, so wisdom is unlocked by a simple but sincere request. For the Bible says, "If any of you lacks wisdom, you should ask God ... and it will be given to you" (James 1:5). But it is wise to ask with our actions and not merely with our words, because wisdom shall come to those who already are trying to live wisely.

Wisdom requires humility, since it's given from above rather than generated from within. As the Bible says, "Do not be wise in your own eyes" (Proverbs 3:7). Indeed, we should not be wise in our own eyes lest we stop looking for wisdom elsewhere. But we should look, since there is so much more that we do not know, and so much more that we can do with what we already know.

For the light of wisdom is like the light of heaven. We can all see the stars as they are, but not so many of us see the stars for what they can be. For how many stargazers can behold in them the constellations they form? And amongst these, who can see in the constellations the navigation they can enable: for the many courses that have been taken and the numerous fortunes that have been forged? So let us not stop with the wisdom that we already know; let us instead become wise with that wisdom, becoming like the mariners who traversed the world because they knew how to chart the sky.

Application: Identify an area or relationship in your life where you do not act as wise as the wisdom you know.

Supplication: God, help me to see how little wisdom I possess while also being that much wiser with the bit of wisdom in my possession. Come, Holy Spirit. Amen.

31

Yes, This Will Be on the Test

Consider it pure joy …
whenever you face trials.

James 1:2

It would be nice to think that faith can save us from every evil, but faith is what saves us for everlasting good. There always has been and always will be challenges that test who we are and what we believe. But we should not be too quick to say that this loss or that bad luck is a test from heaven, as though all the ordeals we face are the same in nature as those faced by someone like Abraham. For much of what happens is just life doing what life does. As Annie Dillard observed, "God is no more blinding people with glaucoma, or testing them with diabetes, or purifying them with spinal pain … than He is jimmying floodwaters or pitching tornadoes at towns."[1]

So the purpose of this particular reflection isn't to resolve the problem of evil but to help us find resolve in the midst of this problem. For while God knows how faithful we'd be beforehand, none of us know how faithful we'll be when trouble is at hand. But when we're facing life's difficulties, we should remember that life is only lived one day at a time. In fact, not a day, an hour, or even a minute—but a moment at a time. So when we're beset by an illness or a fear, take courage in the fact that we never suffer from something for more than a moment at any given point—that we only need enough faith to fill up the split seconds.

Furthermore, to worry today about tomorrow's troubles is like dressing for tomorrow's weather today. It not only does us little good; it can also do us great harm. For worry (as opposed to mere planning or concern) is how we indirectly suffer evils that we've not yet directly experienced—suffering evils we're not even guaranteed we'll encounter. Hence Jesus' wise admonition, "Do not worry about tomorrow, for tomorrow will worry about itself. Each day has enough trouble of its own" (Matthew 6:34).

Indeed, we should not worry, since our fears make God look fearsome and our worry makes us mistake our own travails for actual trials. Let us also not become too afraid, because as Paul said, "God is faithful; he will not let you be [burdened] beyond what you can bear" (1 Corinthians 10:13). (But let it be said we still might bear more than we thought imaginable.)

God does not speak our pain into being, but he can speak to our being through pain. As C. S. Lewis wrote, "God whispers to us in our pleasures, speaks to us in conscience, but shouts in our pain."[2] And perhaps God is trying to tell us—especially through our trials—that we don't need to prove our strength so much as realize our weakness. That it's not about what our faith can stand but the fact that we can fall—directly into the arms of God. "Come to me," as Jesus said, "you who are weary and burdened, and I will give you rest" (Matthew 11:28).

Application: To see how our strength can fail us but grace can save us, watch the film *Shadowlands,* which is about C. S. Lewis and his short-lived life with Joy Davidman.

Supplication: Lord, I need your strength, not merely to be strong but also to be weak. For I cannot be saved so long as I am trying to save myself. Grant me the grace of accepting from you the very things that I was trying to offer to you, such as my love, my life, my virtue, and my strength. Come, Holy Spirit. Amen.

32

Faith for Riches, Faith for Ruin

I count everything as loss because of the surpassing
worth of knowing Christ Jesus my Lord.

Philippians 3:8 ESV

The natural world is filled with scientific and mathematical laws. There are laws that govern motion and laws for thermodynamics, and there are electrostatic laws and gravitational laws; there are laws for everyone and everything. So naturally we might also think that there are spiritual laws that regulate the supernatural realm of life. And those who place Scripture under a microscope to find such laws usually find what they are looking for. To the merciful, the Scriptures show mercy, to the law abiding it looks law giving, and for those in search of guarantees—that faith can win health and wealth or power and protection—they can find a guarantor.

The latter outlook is wisely disparaged but widely desired. For it is inherently human to hope that faith can render rewards, revive health, and overcome obstacles. It's a desire we do not often state explicitly, but one we often pray implicitly—because we live in a world where necessities are commodities and where health counts for more than happiness. Indeed, such motives are entirely plausible, and their precedents are ostensibly scriptural. One need only look at Jabez and Job to see such blessings either sought or bestowed.

It is true that Job's faith was rewarded. But it was not rewarded as we might think. Certainly, having faithfully endured unimaginable hardships, "the LORD restored his fortunes and gave him twice as much as he had before" (Job 42:10). But the reward wasn't his redoubled health and wealth. In fact, these apparent rewards were given not because Job's faith had unlocked the inherent power of belief or discovered the laws of divine reciprocity, but when Job had enough faith to go without them. They came when Job was content enough to see them all go, because the highest good now mattered more to him than every other good—making faith its own reward.

The one law of faith is that it must be led by the law of love. To have the kind of faith that can move mountains, we must love the God of miracles more than the miracles of God. Indeed, we must have faith enough to remain faithful even when the mountains do not move. For miracles are gratuities, not guarantees. Yet we can give to God the miracle of our own faith—and in giving, find that we shall receive. Because as Jesus said, "Seek first the kingdom of God ... and all these things will be added to you" (Matthew 6:33 ESV).

Application: Make a list of the things that you desire from God. Is it equal to or greater than your desire for God?

Supplication: Heavenly Father, please help me to worship you for who you are, not just for what you can do. And when your gifts do not seem to abound, grant me the singular gift of still abiding in you. Come, Holy Spirit. Amen.

33

What Is Faith?

I pray … that Christ may dwell in your hearts
through faith. And I pray that you, being rooted and
established in love, may have power … to grasp how
wide and long and high and deep is the love of Christ,
and to know this love that surpasses knowledge.

Ephesians 3:16–19

So what is this faith?
It's a feeling
For sure

A sense of confidence
About things
In heaven

A sense of assurance
About things
On earth

But it's also a belief
In love, believed
By loving

A love that extends
Above oneself
For God

A love that reaches
From oneself
To others

A love that abides
In oneself for
One's self

Application: Read and pray your way through 1 Corinthians 13.

Supplication: Lord, please deepen my faith, not necessarily by helping me to believe more intensely, but through helping me to love more intently. Come, Holy Spirit. Amen.

34

How to Tell the Time

Teach us to number our days,
that we may gain a heart of wisdom.

Psalm 90:12

Time, not money, is the real currency of this world. Yet we rarely invest our time as wisely as we do our money, despite the fact that what we do with it ultimately determines what we shall do with ourselves. To the contrary, as Seneca observed, "People are frugal in guarding personal property; but as soon as it comes to squandering time they are most wasteful of the one thing in which it is right to be stingy."[1]

Indeed, we spend our time with little appreciation of the fact that how we spend it now influences how it shall be spent for all eternity. So we scatter our hours like seeds in the wind—in work and play, friends and family, sleep and sloth—without much regard for the seeds we plant in our very own souls.

Each day is a day that God has decided to give to us, and

each day is a day that we can determine to give back to God. That does not mean, however, that every day should resemble Sunday, or that we necessarily have to spend less time working so we can spend more time worshiping. God knows that we need to do these other things—like shopping and exercising or reading and socializing—but we need to know that God can do these other things with us. Because God is present in those who have the presence of mind to welcome him, and God hears the inward prayers of those who are outwardly working, and God blesses those who are trying to bless others.

Each day is also a decision about how we can give ourselves back to God. The Bible suggests, "Rejoice always, pray continually, [and] give thanks in all circumstances" (1 Thessalonians 5:16–18). But it is hard to pray and abide throughout the day unless, like Jesus, we begin the day early with prayer and abiding (as it plants the seeds of devotion inside of us, which then grow into completion throughout the day). But it is hard to even do that without reading e-mails before we read the Bible, or thinking about work before we think about God. But perhaps we should try, since we have no hope of giving to God an entire day if we can't give to him a single hour.

Whether we're morning people or not, the Bible does say, "Joy comes with the morning" (Psalm 30:5 ESV). The joy, however, is mutual. For as much as we enter into God, we also get to entertain God. We can literally give God the time of day, allowing him to quietly dwell within an undivided heart. Naturally, we might feel divided about abiding in prayer when distractions are abounding, but we'll soon discover the dividends of being our own timekeepers. For the way we spend our time becomes the only life that we can live, and there is a big difference between truly living and merely being alive.

Application: Wake up half an hour earlier in order to read and pray. When you go to bed the night before, kneel by your bedside and pray for the Holy Spirit to awaken you in the morning with sufficient energy and resolve.

Supplication: Lord, I pray that you shall rise with me; otherwise, I am unlikely to rise for you. Please bless me with a restful night, so I might rest in you tomorrow morning. Come, Holy Spirit. Amen.

35

Faithful with Little, Faithful with Much

> "One who is faithful in a very little
> is also faithful in much."
>
> *Luke 16:10* ESV

Hippocrates remarked that art is long and life is short. And certainly, beauty has a long shelf life and living a short half-life; but "life," Seneca said, "is long if you know how to use it."[1] There is sufficient time to both live well and to work hard, to love much and to build something beautiful.

To have a hobby is part of being human, because we are born with more potential than will ever be employable. But the fact that we can't always pursue our passions professionally—like painting or coaching, writing or woodworking—shouldn't prohibit us from pursuing them purposefully. For there are wondrous things to be done and meaningful accomplishments to be won, so long as we're willing to work hard in our free time—even if it becomes costly.

Each of us is entrusted with certain talents. These might not be unique in quality or unparalleled in quantity, but they can be utilized toward a higher good. So let us love our neighbor with what we love to do, because God has given us various talents—like an aptitude for arithmetic or the ability for leadership—not with the expectation that we should all become successful, but with the intention that we should all be faithful.

It is a great legacy to leave behind something rather than nothing—to build a body of work with somebody else in mind and commit to a craft that can provide both edification and enjoyment. So just as a cathedral is built stone by stone and year by year, we should also build something meal by meal, song by song, and game by game into a sanctuary that shall exist for the sake of somebody else. Let us have little concern for our success or failure, but only concern ourselves with the faithfulness we are to render. For so long as the Lord builds with the builders, the laborers shall not labor in vain.

Time for such endeavors is seldom found, but it can be made. For who cannot spare five minutes a day, which amounts to more than a hundred days in a lifetime? Or who cannot awaken an hour earlier in order to live and love an hour more? Yet there is no guarantee that somebody, or anybody, will appreciate the love and work that we attempt or even accomplish. But our aim is to be ever faithful, regardless of whether we shall ever be successful. It is to hear the words from heaven, "Well done, my good and faithful servant" (Matthew 25:23 NLT).

Application: Brainstorm three ways that you can be purposeful in your pastime.

Supplication: Lord, work with me so that I might work for you, by helping me to love others with what I love to do. Come, Holy Spirit. Amen.

36

The Lord's Prayer

Pray in the Spirit at all times
and on every occasion.

Ephesians 6:18 NLT

Just as there is a Golden Rule, so there is also a golden prayer. It is, of course, the Lord's Prayer—God's own prayer. And while it isn't an exclusive prayer, having to be prayed at the expense of all the others, it is the most inclusive one. As St. Augustine wrote, "If you run through all the words of the holy prayers, I do not think you will find anything in them that is not contained and included in the Lord's Prayer."[1] It's also a prayer best said persistently and passionately but not thoughtlessly. So it's to that end we might read the following thoughts—to help us pray more thoughtfully.

OUR FATHER WHO ART IN HEAVEN. That we have not only a father in heaven, but an Abba Father—a Dad. The kind of dad that is not only the perfect image of paternity, but whose fatherhood is more tender, encouraging, and constant than we can even dare imagine.

HALLOWED BE THY NAME. That if thy name is sacred, how much more thy love? For thou art love—and we are truly loved indeed.

THY KINGDOM COME. THY WILL BE DONE ON EARTH, AS IT IS IN HEAVEN. That before we seek your will regarding corporations and organizations, or cultures and current trends, might we look to the hard work of our own obedience rather than that of others.

GIVE US THIS DAY OUR DAILY BREAD. That we need only have faith enough for today, so long as we have hope enough for tomorrow. That in the hierarchy of trust, it should be easier—not harder—to trust God for something as simple as food to eat and money to buy it, compared to something so staggering as our eternal salvation.

AND FORGIVE US OUR TRESPASSES, AS WE FORGIVE THOSE WHO TRESPASS AGAINST US. That we probably need forgiveness for the paltry nature of our own forgiving, because we often indulge the phantom pains of healed wounds—creating new pains that have to be forgiven again (only it's us who really need the forgiveness).

AND LEAD US NOT INTO TEMPTATION. That we should not be left to our own devices, for the devil has little work to do when we're left alone, if only because we're so quick to do our own dirty work.

BUT DELIVER US FROM EVIL. That we're delivered not just from evil, nor into good, but into our Father's arms and our Dad's delight.

Application: Contemplate the above chapter while listening to Sir John Tavener's "The Lord's Prayer."

Supplication: Lord, when I pray your prayer, may I pray with the help of your Spirit. For when I pray these words on my own, I often feel alone; but when I pray these words with you, I always feel like I am praying to you. Come, Holy Spirit. Amen.

37

Contemplation Lows

May my meditation be pleasing to him.

Psalm 104:34 ESV

We often think that in order to contemplate, we have to turn aside from others before we can turn ourselves to God. That like monks in the desert, we should be hermits in our own homes, because it is only apart from the world that we can find that which lives above it. And this outlook is not totally wrong, as Jesus did say, "When you pray, go into your room, close the door and pray to your Father" (Matthew 6:6). But it's not altogether right, since the road to heaven winds its way alongside other people, and we can't turn upward in faith without turning outward in love, for that is the way of Jesus.

The mystical ascent of men and women must follow the path that Jesus made for them. But that path does not lead straight to heaven, as Jesus did not ascend there without first stopping here. For it was outside the tomb that the risen Jesus told Mary Magdalene, "Do not hold on to me, for I have not yet ascended to the Father" (John 20:17). Indeed, it was there that love bade Jesus stay a while—not due to a lack of love for the Father, but due to the Father's love for us. A love made all the more remarkable, since the Apostles' Creed states that Jesus first descended into hell, which means, having been in hell, the choice to tarry with us here delayed his much-anticipated ascent into heaven.

The fact that Jesus made time for us means that we must make time for others. This means that there is no devotional time so sacred—no prayer so profound, no reading so revelatory, and no praise so pure—that it cannot be interrupted in order to discharge the duties of love, should a valid need arise or an unavoidable occasion occur. For the path upward must lead us outward, which is why Thomas Merton said, "The worst illusion in the life of contemplation would be to try to find God by barricading yourself inside your own soul."[1]

To pray is devout, but to love is divine. So the next time that we are praying and get interrupted because someone needs our assistance, remember that the purpose of prayer is to become purposeful in our love. So, as Søren Kierkegaard said, "When you open the door which you shut in order to pray to God, the first person you meet as you go out is your neighbor whom you shall love."[2] But also know that our neighbors are like living icons, that meeting with them is like meeting with God. Because the God to whom we pray is the God that is hidden—or hopes to hide—within our neighbor's heart.

Indeed, as C. S. Lewis wrote, "Next to the Blessed Sacrament itself, your neighbor is the holiest object presented to your senses."[3] So it should not surprise us when contemplation harkens us back into community, because the God that we would like to find apart from others would himself like to be found amongst them. And yet, it is precisely by finding God in one another that we can then find God within ourselves; because, as the Bible says, "No one has ever seen God; but if we love one another, God lives in us and his love is made complete in us" (1 John 4:12).

Application: The next time you are interrupted by someone while praying, consider the possibility that a short prayer with love enough for someone else is more pleasing to God than a longer prayer with only enough love for him.

Supplication: Lord, help me to see that just as you visit us in the guise of the hungry, the naked, and the poor, so this could also be you knocking at my door. Come, Holy Spirit. Amen.

38

Don't Worry About It

"Do not worry about your life."
Matthew 6:25

Spring is the most graceful season because its beauty appears effortless. Consider, for instance, the birds of the air: how geese migrate thousands of miles without a flight plan and robins build nests without any architectural designs. Regard the fragrance of a lilac and the unfurling of a lily: how they show the beauty of creation as it becomes what it was created to be. Indeed, "every sound you hear is an expression of nature's attentiveness to [God]," Søren Kierkegaard wrote, "which is why you can hear God in it."[1]

The lives of saints are like those of animals, because they seem to have an innate faith as creatures that their Creator will somehow provide for whatever needs they require. For the rest of us, however, our faith seems comparatively inane, since we're still not sure that an infinite divinity would be interested in our finite triviality. In fact, this can seem so insane that we'd rather pay than pray for our daily bread, and depend on Social Security before divine surety. Yet the saints live as we were made to, and do so quite contentedly, while the rest of us live as we would like to, and are quietly discontented. So there must be great truth in the fact that we both imminently and ultimately "live and move and have our being [in God]" (Acts 17:28).

Jesus wants us to not worry about being human, which is to say to not worry about being unfulfilled and incomplete. Instead, Jesus says, "My grace is sufficient for you, for my power is made perfect in weakness" (2 Corinthians 12:9). The challenge, however, is not necessarily believing this, but depending on it. For there's nothing that difficult in believing God's trustworthy; the difficulty is actually trusting in God. We'd rather entrust ourselves to something we can see than someone we cannot. Which isn't to say we have no faith; it's that we're afraid we might lose what faith we do have. This is because trust is often accompanied by the fear that a negative proves a negation—that the lack of God's assistance might disprove God's existence.

But God would like us to go all in, since he wants to be our all in all. This kind of trust, however, is grown, not given. Grace is what makes it possible, not pleasing. So we must choose to trust in the oasis beyond the desert and the peak atop the mountain. But we can trust in God—not necessarily for the sake of a reward—but with the reassurance that there will be one. For the more we can give to God, the more God can give to us. "Whoever can be trusted with very little," Jesus said, "can also be trusted with much" (Luke 16:10).

Application: List the top three sources of worry and concern in your life. Pick one of these and begin the long but liberating process of "letting go and letting God."

Supplication: Heavenly Father, until you are everything to me, it can seem so hard to give anything to you. Indeed, I hardly have the trust to be any more trusting, or the love to be that much more loving. So please accomplish in me that which I cannot accomplish for you. Come, Holy Spirit. Amen.

39

To Get and to Give

"Whoever believes in me will do the works
I have been doing, and they will do even
greater things than these."

John 14:12

Jesus said, "Nothing will be impossible for you" (Matthew 17:20). Yet there are a plethora of plausible things that seem far from possible for us. Likewise, Jesus said that if we have faith as small as a seed, we could tell something as large as a mountain, "'Move from here to there,' and it will move" (Matthew 17:20). But who amongst us can really move the mountains of existence—and tell things like hate and mayhem or death and disease where to go and what to do?

At the heart of our faith is God's faithfulness. So it isn't necessary to work our faith into a frenzy when the only faith that has inherent power is God's faithfulness. Indeed, the size of our belief matters less than simply believing in the size of our God. Which is not to imply that who we are and what we do amounts to nothing, only that in the end it is God alone who forms and fathoms, saves and sustains, gives and takes away. In fact, when it comes to the life of all things, whether they're material or miraculous, "it's not the one who plants or the one who waters who is at the center of this process but God, who makes things grow" (1 Corinthians 3:7 MSG).

Faith is not about what we can do; it's about what God can do. It does not balance human probabilities with divine possibilities, but weighs in with God—or waits upon him. Furthermore, true faith recognizes that we must accept something on faith before we can accomplish the same thing with faith. To doubt historic miracles, for instance, such as those performed by the prophets, doubtlessly precludes us from experiencing them at present. Because as Jesus said, "If they do not listen to Moses and the Prophets, they will not be convinced even if someone rises from the dead" (Luke 16:31).

When we believe in the miracles of the Bible, we are in a position to receive biblical miracles. Likewise, when we have enough faith to get such astonishing and supernatural assistance, we also have faith enough to give that kind of support to others. For this was always the divine intention: that our capacity to receive miracles becomes the same capability to perform them. That believing in the miracle of prayer, we can pray for others; by trusting in God's provision, we can also provide for others; and knowing that our infirmities shall be healed, we can attend to the injuries of others.

Application: Just as we look to God for miracles, so God looks to us for the miraculous. To that end, try talking to someone about the hopes and dreams and desperate desires they might harbor regarding miraculous assistance.

Supplication: Jesus, as much as I might pray to receive miracles, I should also pray to render them—especially the mundane but meaningful miracles associated with kindness, service, forgiveness, and generosity. So I ask that I shall give for you with the same eagerness with which I have sought to receive these things from you. Come, Holy Spirit. Amen.

40

Not Experiencing God

In him you too are being built together to
become a dwelling in which God lives by his Spirit.

Ephesians 2:22

People are often told that if they have faith in Jesus, they will most certainly experience closeness with Christ—that they will discover a level of intimacy and degree of fulfillment beyond their greatest expectations. But this is not entirely true.

Faith is what enables God to have these experiences with us, while grace is what allows us to have such experiences with God. It is important to note, therefore, that while one is a necessity, the other is only a gratuity. Because it's essential that God should be at home in our hearts in order for us to become at home in heaven. But it is not necessary for us to feel close to God in order to have faith in God.

The fact that we do not always feel God's presence does not mean that God is not always present. God is ever present, and therefore never needs to be found. Instead, we need to be found, and faith is what makes us findable. For it is we who struggle with abiding in God when God seems like he's not residing in us. And we are the ones who—struggling with life or dealing with death—charge the Lord with having a closed heart but do so little to open our own.

But there is great faith in the heart that remains open amidst real turmoil. For the greatest faith we can have comes when we feel as though we have no faith at all but still desire to make God happy in our hearts, rather than demand that God first gladden our own.

It is liberating to know that whether or not we feel like we're in a relationship with God, our faithfulness can ensure that God feels as if he's in a relationship with us. Likewise, it's encouraging that the greatest gift we have to give is the only gift that we can give—for who we are is all we can offer. So let's give ourselves to God, with the awareness that we neither give as we've been given to, nor do we give without being given to. For it's only by grace, and not our goodness, that our hearts can become a happy hearth and home.

Grace gives to us—and us alone—the freedom to give our hearts back to God, because God will not take them. He can act forcefully upon our hearts, but he shall not forcefully enter them. Instead, God knocks upon our doors and waits to be welcomed with faith, hope, and love. He also knocks as the lonely, longing to be let in; as the needy, in need of provision; and as the unlovable, longing to be loved. Indeed, God knocks with everyone and everything, hoping we shall answer—however loveless, faithless, or even clueless we might feel—so others can also experience the God that lives inside of us.

Application: While listening to Arvo Pärt's "Spiegel im Spiegel (Violin and Piano)," read, reread, and ponder Matthew 15:31–46.

Supplication: Lord, since I cannot determine the depth to which I presently experience you, but I can decide the degree to which you experience me, I pray that you shall help me to welcome you—along with many others—into a heart that is filled with faith, hope, and love. Come, Holy Spirit. Amen.

Conclusion

No one who hopes in you
will ever be put to shame.
Psalm 25:3

This conclusion does not aim at clarification, but reiteration. It is a simple restating of the book's main themes. And the ordering of these phrases is not important—they're just words to help us along in the way of faith:

Faith does not ensure that we shall experience God at present, but it ensures that God shall experience us presently.

The primary purpose of this life is to be known by God. To then know God as we have been known is the principal reward of the next life.

The knowledge of us that God seeks is not so much rational as relational, because it's based on intimacy with us rather than information about us.

The life of faith lives through love. It is a love that extends upward, outward, and inward: a belief in love—which is believed by loving.

Faith requires doctrines no less than traveling needs directions. But our doctrinal integrity should not undermine the integral nature of our love for one another.

The language of faith is prayer. But we are most fluent in prayer not when we get what we want, but when God gets what he wants.

Doubt is not the failure of our faith, but the occasion for it. And when we feel further away from God, our faithfulness enables God to feel that much closer to us.

Faith must be lived individually, but it cannot be lived independently. The faithful are to keep faith with one another.

How we live our lives becomes the only lives that we live. So let us value our time and remember that our lives are only as large as our love.

Grace is what makes faith possible, not necessarily pleasant. But faith can be made more enjoyable—and more animated—by developing a deepening sense of gratitude.

We need faith enough not only to move mountains, but also to remain faithful when the mountains do not move.

When it comes to using our talents and investing our time, we do not have to be successful so long as we are trying to be faithful.

Live well and sin wisely. For there are some vices—like envy and worry—that come with all of the pain and none of the pleasure. By all means, we should try not to be sinful at all, since it is wrong to sin, but know that it is even worse to sin stupidly.

The most important thing about faith is not what we can do, but what God can do. Indeed, not just what God can do, but what God has done and will do.

It is my sincere desire that *The Way of Faith* will help everyone to love God above themselves, because God has loved us with all of himself. So if there are any errors in this book, please forgive me—and remember that my goal has always been good, that it has always been God. But it is my supreme confidence that such a hope shall not be put to shame, because I believe, as Thomas Merton wrote, that "the desire to please you [O God], does in fact please you."[1] But let me now draw this conclusion to its close. For there comes a time when there is nothing more to say—there are only things to do.

THE WAY OF FAITH:
A Reading List

Read not to contradict and confute;
nor to believe and take for granted;
nor to find talk and discourse;
but to weigh and consider.
—*Francis Bacon*, Of Studies[1]

Reading is like a party: the more the merrier. It would be a great shame, therefore, if you were to end this book without getting to know many more books. So please consider the following titles as worthwhile—indeed, far worthier—successors to *The Way of Faith*. For these books will add to one's enjoyment of life and appreciation for being alive. They shall bless you as they have blessed me: some with wisdom, others with clarity, and so many with charity. Only do be careful to not mistake your spiritual reading for your spiritual life. Because, as Marcel Proust rightly cautioned, "Reading is on the threshold of the spiritual life; it can introduce us to it, but it does not constitute it."[2] To live a spiritual life requires faith, hope, and love, not merely C. S. Lewis, Thomas à Kempis, or even the Bible.

The Road to Character by **David Brooks**

How can we talk about good and evil, or holiness and sin, in a world that either cringes at these words or is clueless about them? Well, to begin with, we might read this illuminating and inspiring book about the formation of character. Written by David Brooks—one of the most perceptive and considerate columnists of the *New York Times*—this book is both a fresh take on an ancient school of wisdom, as well as a modern guidebook on how to talk about moral things that really matter.

The Alphabet of Grace by **Frederick Buechner**

Frederick Buechner is one of the most humane, sympathetic, and soul-searching novelists and nonfiction writers that the past half century has produced. In *The Alphabet of Grace*, he opens a window into his own life and invites us to see in the course of a single day the ways in which faith can find God in the meaningful but mundane things, especially when one's faith seems outmatched by the things that are more formidable.

The Divine Milieu by **Pierre Teilhard de Chardin**

Sometimes it feels like our faith has to be otherworldly in order to be faithful in a world where matter and not miracles seems to hold sway. But *The Divine Milieu* is beautiful for how this-worldly it is, reminding us that it's "by means of all created things, without exception, the divine assails us, penetrates us, and molds us. We imagined it as distant and inaccessible, whereas in fact we live steeped in its burning layers."[3]

Orthodoxy by G. K. Chesterton

What we believe in matters as much as or more than the act of merely believing. So we should seek to understand our faith just as much as our faith should be seeking understanding. So I highly recommend Chesterton's romping, rambling, raucous, and resplendent classic, *Orthodoxy*. For this book can bring our faith to light and to life.

Holy the Firm by Annie Dillard

Holy the Firm is a short but far from superficial look into the mystery of life: the kind of mystery that includes everything from natural beauty to what seems like divine cruelty. It explores the world and how God lives within it—and can appear outside of it—but invites us to live in this world more wilfully and aware than ever before.

The Story of Christianity, Volume I & II by Justo L. González

You cannot understand a religion without knowing its history. And for those who do not know the history of Christianity, this book is a perfect place to start. It is simultaneously scholarly and readable while also enjoyable and erudite.

The Reason for God by Timothy Keller

This book is no *Orthodoxy* or *Mere Christianity*, but then again, the twentieth century is no substitute for the twenty-first. In order to be intellectually equipped for having faith in the postmodern world, we need a book (and many more) from this century, not just the past one. And Tim Keller's *The Reason for God* is just such a book: intelligent, intelligible, and deeply rooted in both faith and reason.

Works of Love by **Søren Kierkegaard**

You cannot undertake faith without love, and you cannot understand love as well as you could without this book. That is not to say that this book is easily understandable—it's Søren Kierkegaard that we're talking about—but for those with both the heart and mind to read it, I can personally guarantee they shall never read anything else like it.

The Mystery of Marriage by **Mike Mason**

I do not know what it is like to be married, but I hope that should I become a married man, I shall have the same kind of faithfulness to my partner and an equal admiration for the institution of marriage as Mike Mason does. Till then, his book can teach me and countless others about the true nature of faithfulness itself, including the faith we owe God and the faithfulness we constantly receive from him.

New Seeds of Contemplation and *Contemplative Prayer* by **Thomas Merton**

These two books abound with insight, integrity, and intelligence. But while they are not as helpful as we might like in teaching us how to pray contemplatively, they are very helpful at teaching us how to think clearly about contemplation. Furthermore, both of these books provide endless and perceptive insights into who we are when we pray and to whom it is we are praying.

Christ & Culture by **H. Richard Niebuhr**

It is all too easy to assume that your faith represents the only way of being faithful. But the richness of Christ and the complexity of the world have conspired to create multiple faith-based approaches. And in this landmark study—as relevant today as it was when it was published in 1951—Niebuhr does as good a job as anyone in helping us to understand who we are, what we believe, how we behave, and why all of us do this so differently from one another.

A Prayer Journal by Flannery O'Connor

This is a short book that might only appeal to fans of Flannery O'Connor's fantastic and fearsome fiction. But it is nevertheless a fascinating study into faith and art. For it shows a young artist grappling with her art, and a future saint at odds with her faith.

Knowing God by J. I. Packer

As much as I have focussed on God knowing us, I do not want to give the impression that we cannot know God. There is much to know, and much knowing to be done. To that end, you can read this tried and true classic by J. I. Packer.

Gilead by Marilynne Robinson

Robinson is a world-class novelist and the leading light of American letters. So it's no surprise that her Pulitzer Prize-winning novel, *Gilead*, should be a profound and penetrating study of human life as lived in the small town of Gilead, Iowa. It is also a deeply moving portrait of grace and faith through the various stages of childhood, adulthood, and life's later years.

Authentic Faith by Gary Thomas

The most beautiful thing about this book is not the fact that Thomas accurately portrays the attributes of authentic faith; it's how Thomas inspires us—through contemporary stories and classical wisdom—to actually be so authentic as to have faith.

Becoming Human by Jean Vanier

In this astonishing book, Jean Vanier, founder of L'Arche, teaches us how to really keep faith with one another in a community. He shows us the importance of uniting those who are seemingly strong with those who are ostensibly weak, because we cannot become fully human until we realize the strength in other people's weakness, and the weaknesses hidden within our very own strengths.

The Shaming of the Strong by Sarah Williams

This book tells the intimate, agonizing, and ultimately uplifting tale of a harrowing pregnancy and the short-lived life of a much-loved child. In this book Sarah—and her husband, Paul—shine the light of hidden dignity and hard-won faith in what is surely one of life's darkest times. It is a testimony to true faith and a story of God's abiding faithfulness.

Acknowledgments

Thank you to everyone who has contributed to the making, breaking, and remaking of this book. In particular, I'd like to express my sincerest gratitude to my parents, Peter and Joanne. Likewise, I wish to thank everyone at BroadStreet, from top to bottom, for making this project possible. I'd also like to acknowledge the much-appreciated assistance of my agent, Dan Balow, as well as thank my good friends, David John Parker and Richard Kelly Kemick, for their editorial assistance. To the rest of my family and all of my friends, let me say just how highly I value your love, enthusiasm, prayers, and support. But most of all, I thank my God for the opportunity to give to him—not just my best—but my all.

Notes

Seeking Spiritual Spring

1 Thomas Merton, *Contemplative Prayer* (New York: Doubleday, 1996), 83.

2 Frederick Buechner, *The Sacred Journey* (New York: HarperCollins, 1982), 112.

Devotion 2

1 Leo Tolstoy, *A Confession* (New York: Penguin, 2008), 58.

Devotion 3

1 Martin Luther King Jr., *Strength to Love* (Minneapolis: Augsburg Fortress, 2010), 47.

Devotion 7

1 Marilynne Robinson, *The Givenness of Things* (Toronto: HarperCollins, 2015), 4.

2 Thomas Merton, *No Man Is an Island* (New York: Harcourt, 1983), 238.

Devotion 8

1 T. S. Eliot, "East Coker," *The Complete Poems and Plays* (London: Faber and Faber, 2004), V, 35.

Devotion 9

1 Thomas à Kempis, *The Imitation of Christ* (New York: Vintage, 1998), 14.

2 John Simpson, *The Oxford Dictionary of Proverbs*, 5th ed. (Oxford: Oxford University Press, 2008), 337.

3 Kempis, *The Imitation of Christ*, 212.

Devotion 10

1 A commonly attributed saying of John Wesley.

2 Cicero, *Pro Plancio* (London: Forgotten Books, 2016), section 80.

Devotion 13

1 Elizabeth Knowles, ed., *Oxford Concise Dictionary of Quotations*, 4th ed. (Oxford: Oxford University Press, 2011), 370.

2 Joseph de Maistre, *The Executioner* (New York: Penguin, 2009), 34.

Devotion 14

1 Merton, *Contemplative Prayer*, 83.

Devotion 16

1 Thomas à Kempis, *The Imitation of Christ* (New York: Penguin, 2013), 5.

Devotion 18

1 St. Bernard of Clairvaux, *Oxford Concise Dictionary of Quotations*, 32.

Devotion 20

1 Tolstoy, *A Confession*, 12.

2 John Locke, *An Essay concerning Human Understanding* (1690).

Devotion 24

1 William Blake, "The Clod and the Pebble," in *Songs of Experience* (1794).

Devotion 25

1 C. S. Lewis, *The Screwtape Letters*, in *The Complete C. S. Lewis Signature Classics* (New York: HarperCollins, 1996), 206.

2 Ibid., 208.

3 Lucretius, *Life and Mind* (New York: Penguin, 2005), 2.

Devotion 26

1 Friedrich Nietzsche, *Man Alone with Himself* (New York: Penguin, 2008), 12.

Devotion 28

1 Leszek Kołakowski, "The Devil in History," *Encounter*, January 1981, quoted in Tony Judt, *Reappraisals* (New York: Penguin, 2009), 135.

2 Lewis, *The Screwtape Letters*, in *The Complete C. S. Lewis Signature Classics*, 183.

3 Roy F. Baumesiter and John Tierney, *Willpower* (New York: Penguin, 2011), 51.

Devotion 29

1 Robert Frost, "Nothing Gold Can Stay" (1923).

2 Pierre Teilhard de Chardin, *The Divine Milieu* (Toronto: R. P. Pryne, 2015), Kindle edition, location 1330.

Devotion 30

1 Marcel Proust, *Days of Reading* (New York: Penguin, 2008), 70.

Devotion 31

1 Annie Dillard, *For the Time Being* (New York: Vintage, 1999), 167.

2 C. S. Lewis, *The Problem of Pain*, in *The Complete C. S. Lewis Signature Classics*, 604.

Devotion 34

1 Seneca, *On the Shortness of Life* (New York: Penguin, 2004), 4.

Devotion 35

1 Seneca, *On the Shortness of Life*, 2.

Devotion 36

1 St. Augustine, quoted in *Catechism of the Catholic Church* (New York: Doubleday, 1997), 727.

Devotion 37

1 Thomas Merton, *New Seeds of Contemplation* (New York: New Directions, 2007), 64.
2 Søren Kierkegaard, *Works of Love* (New York: Harper & Row, 1964), 64.
3 C. S. Lewis, *The Weight of Glory*, in *The Complete C. S. Lewis Signature Classics*, 46.

Devotion 38

1 Søren Kierkegaard, *Spiritual Writings* (New York: HarperCollins, 2010), 201.

Conclusion

1 Thomas Merton, *Thoughts in Solitude* (New York: Farrar, Straus and Giroux, 1958), 79.

Reading List

1 Francis Bacon, *Of Empire* (New York: Penguin, 2005), 85.
2 Proust, *Days of Reading*, 72.
3 De Chardin, *The Divine Milieu*, location 1330.

About the Author

T. W. S. Hunt is an Anglo-Canadian writer, educator, and speaker living near Calgary, Canada. His previous book is entitled *Winter with God*.

He was born in England and immigrated to Canada in 1999. He lives in the foothills of the Rocky Mountains. An avid learner, he studied history at Trinity Western University and the University of Oxford. He later acquired a bachelor of education at the University of British Columbia, and an MA in theological studies from Regent College. He has worked in the Canadian Prime Minister's Office and at *The American Interest* magazine. In his free time, he enjoys hiking, snowshoeing, movies, and spending time with family and friends.

To inquire about booking T. W. S. Hunt for speaking engagements or retreat leadership, please email twshunt. contact@gmail.com. For more information and to stay connected, visit twshunt.com or facebook.com/twshuntauthor.

MORE FROM T.W.S. HUNT

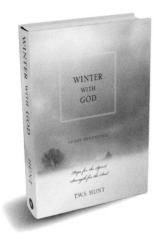

WINTER WITH GOD
Hope for the Spirit,
Strength for the Soul

This 40-day devotional deals much with God's absence as His presence, for it is about the spiritual season of winter—a time when the light faith has dimmed and the warmth love has cooled.

Written with a mystic's heart, scholar's mind, and a poet's pen, Winter with God is a profound meditation on the opportunities and challenges we face when our relationship with God seems dormant, endangered, or simply one-sided.

Suitable for both longtime pilgrims and the newfound faith (or faithless), this rich and compelling devotional about winter with God—a season through which every soul must pass—shows how the hardest season to experience can also be the most rewarding endure.

Discover hope for your spirit and strength for your soul.

(Read an excerpt on the following pages.)

Endorsements

T. W. S. Hunt can write, and he understands his topic. His book will give real help to believers working their way through the winter he describes.

~J. I. PACKER
Theologian and best-selling author of *Knowing God*

T. W. S. Hunt is the best of both worlds—a true writer and a true thinker. He is poetic in his expression, profound in his thought, and biblical in his passion. *Winter with God* displays moments of brilliance and creativity that mark the marvelous debut of a young, up-and-coming writer who deserves to be noticed and read.

~GARY THOMAS
Best-selling author of *Authentic Faith* and *Sacred Marriage*

T. W. S. Hunt has the three qualities I most value in a spiritual writer: honesty, depth, and verve. *Winter with God* crackles with surprising images, a lively play of language, and probing commitment to truth. An auspicious debut from a vibrant new voice!

~MIKE MASON
Author of *The Gospel According to Job*

The combination of rich, poetic writing and practical, forthright questioning makes this book unique. It will warm the hearts of those in winter.

~S. C. WILLIAMS
Author of *The Shaming of the Strong*

Spiritual Winter

> You always expect to be sad … each year when the
> leaves fell from the trees and their branches were bare
> against the wind and the cold, wintry light. But you
> knew there would always be the spring, as you knew
> the river would flow again after it was frozen.
>
> *Ernest Hemingway, A Moveable Feast*[1]

Shakespeare's *Richard III* doesn't say that now is the winter of our *contentment*. Quite the opposite, winter is the season of our "discontent."[2] Winter is the graveyard of the entire year: all of spring, summer, and autumn are buried deep within it. And long after Christmas carols have ceased to be sung, many of us are still singing, "I really can't stay (But, baby, it's cold outside)."[3]

Winter is something we learn to live with and live through. We have to because it lasts a quarter of the calendar year or much longer if, like me, you live in Canada! Still, the season has its charms. As Ralph Waldo Emerson said, "For the attentive eye, each moment of the year has its beauty."[4] In Canada, sunny winter skies unveil themselves in champagne brightness, the air is crisp and fine like cut crystal, and ice turns waterways into highways. Also, the skiing is superb! But more than any other season, winter is one we watch from behind a window. It's the season we long for least, and the one we're least sad to see go.

So too, with our spiritual winters—our days of discontent: when God's divine light rises late and sets early. In such times, nothing seems to grow. Where warmth once abounded, things come to feel frigid. And the landscape of our lives—whether it's felt within or without—appears colorless, formless, and lifeless.

Whereas we can predict a meteorological winter's beginning and end, there's no methodology for when we winter with God. For us, seasons *with* God feel like what time is *to* God. As Peter wrote, "A day is like a thousand years, and a thousand years are like a day" (2 Peter 3:8 NIV). There's simply no telling when winter with God will end. We only know that it will end in this life or the next.

The spiritual work of winter is to survive the cold by keeping warm one's love for God. We mustn't try to avoid this spiritual season—praying, as in Scripture, "that it may not happen in winter" (Mark 13:18). Because it's in winter that we learn to love God out of season, or rather, in spite of the season. It's then that we stop asking *from* God and instead ask *for* God. And in the bleak midwinter, we begin to fathom what it means to love God with all of one's being.

This slim volume of spiritual meditations is wintry in its outlook. It points to the ways in which grace descends upon life, like a soft, quiet snowfall. It wants to walk beside you in the cold and show you the fresh footsteps of Jesus. And it aims to fan dying embers into living flames, to stoke the fires of refinement in order to ignite a life of discipleship. For in this chilly and darkened season, God has given us the gift of fire. Jesus is the spark, and we are the kindling. To keep warm, we must burn with love, and to see far, we must burn very brightly.

This book recommends that we throw everything into the flames—starting with ourselves—so that everything will be illuminated and transformed by the Refiner's fire. But rest assured, we shall neither be scorched nor singed. As the prophet Isaiah promised, "When you walk through the fire you shall not be burned, and the flame shall not consume you" (Isaiah 43:2). The light of the fire is only meant to see us through the winter and the warmth of its blaze to keep us till the spring.

Winter with God is best explored chronologically over the span of days and weeks. This slow and considered approach—reading one chapter at a time—will gradually expose you to the forces of spiritual reformation. Like weathering on a rock, it will reshape you in new and unexpected ways. Into what exactly, or whom, neither the author nor the reader can know. I only hope this book will help you through your spiritual winter. I pray that you will evermore live in God, and God will even more live in you.

Why Do We Pray?

Seek first the kingdom of God and his righteousness,
and all these things will be added to you.

Matthew 6:33

God made reality with prayer in mind. It's an essential part of the infrastructure of everyday life. In fact, prayer is as much (and more) a language of reality as mathematics, chemistry, or physics. The supernatural and the natural are not separate in Christ—for all reality is His reality. As such, God invites us to pray about everything, not as if it were so, but because it is so.

Prayer may seem otherworldly, but it is decidedly this-worldly. If it weren't, Paul wouldn't tell us to "pray without ceasing" (1 Thessalonians 5:17), to "pray in the Spirit at all times" (Ephesians 6:18 NLT), and to "devote ourselves to prayer" (Acts 6:4). For prayer is a reliable resource in so far as we rely on God.

A rich prayer life—or rather, a life of prayer—is not the pinnacle of devotion. It's the foundation. There isn't a saint who's known for not praying or a revival that began without it. So we can't expect further progress in our spiritual lives without substantive prayer. But we can't all be saints, right? Then again, we can't exactly set the bar lower. Christ, whom we're to imitate, rose early and often, in order to pray earnestly and in solitude.

Prayer is only so good at getting what we want. But if we trust God, we're assured we'll get what we need. As Jesus Himself promised, "Your Father knows what you need before you ask him" (Matthew 6:8). Prayer, on the other hand, is excellent at getting what God wants. As 1 John attests, "This is the confidence we have in approaching God: that if we ask anything according to his will, he hears us" (5:14 NIV). So progress in prayer isn't necessarily when we get what we ask for, but when we trust God enough to ask Him for whatever He wants.

Prayer doesn't exclude personal requests, but they aren't its essence. At the heart of prayer, or in the heart of whoever prays, is a crossroads. To the left, we try to change God, and get Him to do things; to the right, we seek to be changed by God, and to do things for Him. One is the way of discipleship, the other isn't. That's not to say we can't ask God for things! Jesus invites us to, and says, "If you ask me anything in my name, I will do it" (John 14:14). But we should examine our prayers and determine *for* whose name are we asking. Do our prayers flow from loving God before ourselves, or for ourselves?

Application: Write a short letter to God, inquiring about what brings Him happiness and satisfaction.

Supplication: Lord, I trust you for what I need; I ask you for what you want. Come, Holy Spirit. Amen.